Amanda **Thomas**

Total
KET
Teacher's Book

▶▶▶ Internet Projects ◀◀◀

On pages 4-33 you will find some enjoyable and informative Internet Projects which learners can complete. There are projects for all fifteen units, each one related to the featured topic of that unit.

To find the correct website:
- go to the Black Cat website **www.blackcat-cideb.com**;
- use the site's search engine to access the page for *Total KET*;
- click on 'project links' and a pop-up window will open;
- all the projects are clearly marked by their page number.

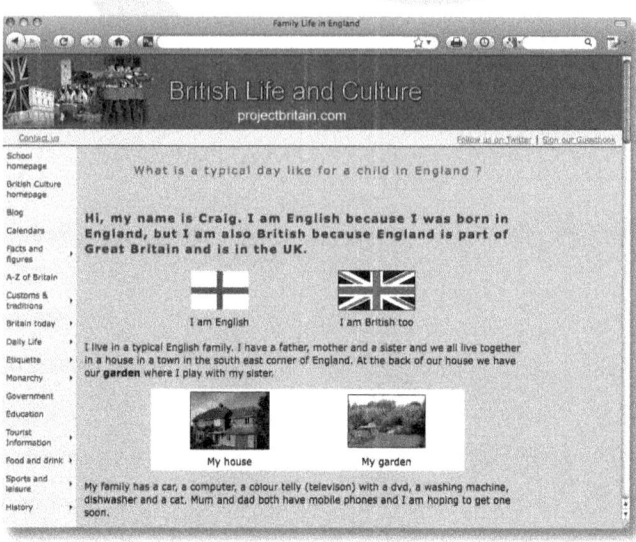

Contents

Unit	Topic	Student's Book: Teaching Notes & Keys	Vocabulary Maximiser: Answer Key:
1	My day	4	39
2	This is my family	6	39
3	Teaching & learning	8	39
4	Rock school	10	40
5	Can you surf?	12	40
6	A piece of cake	14	40
7	Out and about	16	41
8	Be careful!	18	41
9	I need a hat!	20	41
10	What's on?	22	42
11	At home	24	42
12	How much is it?	26	42
13	Mother Nature	28	43
14	She's very funny	30	43
15	I love my city	32	43

Answer Key to the Grammar Bank	34
Answer Key to the Communication Bank	35
Teacher's Book Communication Resource	36
Guide and Answer Key to the Practice Tests	44

Recording Scripts:
Student's Book 47
Skills & Vocab Maximiser 53
Practice Tests 57

Extra Activities 61

Sample Answer Sheets 77

UNIT 1

KET topics	Daily life; Personal identification
Vocabulary	Verb-noun collocations; Telling the time; Days of the week, months, seasons
Grammar	Present Simple: affirmative & negative; Personal pronouns; Prepositions of time
Reading	Understanding personal details
Writing	Introducing yourself: **R&W9** Email
Listening	Everyday activities: **L2** Matching
Speaking	Greetings; Daily routines

Warmer (page 8)

1. Ask the class to look at the information about Scott Walker. In pairs or as a whole class answer the questions. If possible draw/show a map of the UK and get learners to identify Glasgow and Liverpool.
Don't give grammar explanations at this stage – teach *was born* as a set phrase.

   KEY **1** He is 15 years old.
   2 He was born in Glasgow.
   3 He lives in Liverpool.

2. Learners complete the speech bubble individually.

   KEY Open answers

3. Choose an able learner to introduce his/her partner to the class. NB elicit *Her name's...*, *She's... years old*. Get a few more learners to introduce their partner.

   KEY Open answers

4. This is the same task as R&W2. The focus is mainly on lexis rather than grammar. Look at the example as a whole class and check the meaning of *marathon runner*. Explain that likes and dreams are not possible here, you'd need to say, *He would like to be a marathon runner*. Learners complete the sentences in pairs or individually.

   KEY **1**B **2**B **3**C **4**B **5**C

Grammar (page 9)

5. The Grammar Bank section is for learners to refer to while they are doing a grammar exercise in class or for homework, or to check their answers to an activity. Don't read through this with the class. Get learners to complete the table individually or in pairs. They can check their answers by looking at the Grammar Bank. Practise the pronunciation of the contracted forms.

   KEY **1** you're **2** he's **3** she's **4** we're **5** they're **6** you aren't **7** he isn't **8** she isn't **9** we aren't **10** they aren't

6. Elicit the 3rd person forms from the class (they've already seen most of them in ex. 4). With a weaker class, as extra practice, write the base form of the verb on the board, say the pronouns and point to one of the verbs for learners to give the correct form. Do this quickly to keep the pace lively.
Explain that all other verbs form the negative with *don't/doesn't*. NB If learners are familiar with this go straight to ex. 7.

   KEY **1** goes **2** does **3** has **4** gets **5** studies **6** watches

7. Do question 1 as a whole class to check learners understand the task.
Check the answers as a whole class paying attention to the pronunciation of the contracted forms.

   KEY **1** don't **2** doesn't **3** isn't **4** aren't **5** don't **6** isn't

Reading (page 9)

8. The reading activity is preparation for R&W5, (although there isn't a *Doesn't say* option here). Look at the photo and elicit *swimming* and *swimmer*.
Ask learners to read the first paragraph and then complete the sentences about Anna. Then learners read the rest of the text. Encourage them to do this quite quickly. Don't answer questions about vocabulary at this point.

   KEY **1** Anna is 13 years old. **2** She was born in Warsaw, Poland. **3** She lives in London.

9. Learners can work together or do the exercise individually and then check their answers with a partner. Tell them to find and underline the answers in the text.

   KEY **1**T **2**T **3**F **4**T **5**F **6**F

Vocabulary (page 10)

10. This introduces learners to the idea of collocation – certain words which go together. For example in English you can *take/have* a

4

My day

shower (whereas in some other languages you do/make a shower.) Encourage learners to think about what sounds or feels right.

KEY 1 go 2 have 3 go 4 have 5 take 6 go 7 have/make 8 have 9 do 10 do

11 Remind learners to be careful of the negative form before they do ex. 11 – NOT *he doesn't takes*, for example. They can do this individually and then check with a partner. Monitor while learners are working and pick out any problem areas to focus on in feedback.

KEY 1 have 2 does 3 take 4 do 5 goes 6 have

12 Learners will be expected to know both ways to tell the time in English, e.g, *quarter past three* and *three fifteen*. Find out how much the class already knows by eliciting the times on the clocks. If they don't know how to tell the time in English you'll need to go back to the beginning. Start by drawing clock faces on the board (or better using a real/toy clock) showing times.
For extra practice, say some times and get learners to write or draw the times.

KEY 1 half past nine/nine thirty 2 quarter to four/three forty-five 3 quarter past six/six fifteen 4 twenty past ten/ten twenty

13 Learners complete the exercise by writing both ways of saying the time.

KEY 1 half past six/six thirty 2 quarter past eight/eight fifteen 3 quarter to eight/seven forty-five 4 twenty past nine/nine twenty

Grammar (page 10)

14 Check that learners know the days of the week, months and seasons. Page 6 of the Maximiser has exercises on these words. Pay attention to pronunciation.
As a follow-up, get learners to write a sentence using each of the prepositions, e.g. *I get up at half past seven. I don't go to school on Sunday. I was born in January.* etc.

KEY 1 at 2 on 3 in 4 at 5 in

Complete the Rules!

KEY 1 on 2 in 3 at 4 in

Listening (page 11)

(2) See recording script on page 47.

15 This encourages learners to predict the kind of language they may hear in the listening task. This is a useful skill as it helps to prepare them better to 'tune in' to the topic of the conversation. Do this as a whole class brainstorming activity on the board.

KEY *Possible answers*
1 basket, team, player, practice 2 photo, take
3 actor, drama, horror 4 song, practice
5 music, 6 customer, shop assistant

16 Ex. 16 is based on L2. Check learners understand the words in options A-H. Play the recording twice. Learners compare their answers. Play the recording again if necessary or get learners to read the recording script and listen at the same time.

KEY 1G 2D 3H 4F 5E

Speaking (page 11)

17 Do the speaking activity as a mingle. (Don't expect learners to ask questions though as this doesn't come up until unit 2). Learners need to stand up and move around talking to as many classmates as possible. They can simply make statements and write down the name of a learner who does two things at the same time as them. As feedback, find out what time most learners get up, have a shower, etc.

KEY Open answers

Writing (page 11)

18 Learners complete the email with the correct form of the verbs and use this as a model for the writing activity in ex. 19.

KEY 1 is 2 live 3 starts 4 finishes 5 do 6 watch

19 This task is based on R&W9. The focus here is on effective communication not grammatical accuracy and the most important thing is for learners to cover the information in the bullet points.

KEY Sample answer

> Dear Lauren,
> My name is Sophie. I'm 15 years old.
> I go to school at 8.45 and finish at 4.15. After school I do my homework and then I play on the computer!
> Love,
> Sophie

▶▶▶ **Internet Project** ◀◀◀

Read about Asan's day. Are these sentences true or false?
1 Asan gets up early.
2 He takes the bus to school.
3 His lessons start at 9 o'clock.
4 He has lunch at school.
5 He goes to school in the afternoon.
6 He does his homework before dinner.
7 He sees his friends in the evening.

KEY 1T 2T 3F 4F 5F 6T 7F

UNIT 2

KET topics	People; Social interaction
Vocabulary	People in the family; Describing personal appearance
Grammar	Present Simple: questions and short answers; Possessive s; Possessive adjectives
Reading	Introductions: **R&W7** Open cloze
Writing	Families: **R&W9** Email
Listening	**L1** Multiple-choice pictures
Speaking	Asking about families

Warmer (page 12)

1. Ask the class if they are from a big family or a small family. Ask a few students how many brothers and sisters they have.
Encourage learners to make sentences about the family in the picture, e.g. *I think Luke and Harry are brothers. I think Harry is 15.*
Don't try and elicit sentences using the possessive *s* yet.

   KEY Open answers

2. Now get learners to read what Megan says about her family. In pairs they practise describing their own family orally.

   KEY Open answers

Vocabulary (page 12)

3. In pairs learners complete the vocabulary table. Pay attention to pronunciation of *daughter* and *aunt* when doing feedback.

   KEY 1 sister 2 cousin 3 mother 4 mum 5 wife 6 aunt 7 grandmother 8 granddaughter

4. Elicit the plural forms.

   KEY Wife: *wives* is irregular (*man = men, woman = women, child = children* are also irregular).

5. Learners complete the sentences. You can extend this task by getting learners to write more sentences about Megan's family, e.g. *Megan has two cousins. Karen has two daughters.*

   KEY 1 children 2 parents 3 grandparents

Grammar (page 13)

6. Learners match the questions and answers by looking at the picture on page 12. There's no need to explain the grammar before they do this task. Encourage a guided discovery approach. Drill the questions and answers to focus on natural stress and intonation.

   KEY 1A 2D 3E 4B 5C

7. Look at the example together and then refer learners to the Grammar Bank to complete ex. 7. In feedback get one learner to read out the question and another to answer.

   KEY 1 Yes, he is. 2 Yes, they are. 3 No, she doesn't. 4 Yes, she does. 5 No, they don't.

8. Learners complete the questions. You can extend the task by getting them to ask you some questions, e.g. *Do you get up early?*

   KEY 1 Do 2 Is 3 Are 4 Does 5 Do 6 Is

Complete the Rules!

Look at the information about contractions and possessive *s*. Remind learners about the contracted forms of *he is* and *she is*. Look at ex. 6.1 and ask learners if *Megan's* in this question is a contracted form, i.e. *Is Julia Megan is mother?* This should make it clear that *'s* has another function. Refer learners to the Grammar Bank and see if they can identify the different uses of *'s* in sentences 1-3.

   KEY 1 possesive singular 2 contraction of *is* 3 possesive singular, possessive plural, plural noun

9. Look at the sentences and elicit all the possessive adjectives from the class, starting with *she – her, they – their*. Then get the class to match options A-E with sentences 1-5 in pairs.

   KEY 1E 2C 3D 4A 5B

10. Learners write five sentences about their families. This can be done for homework if time is short. Get learners to read the Grammar Bank again at home and complete the exercises there to help consolidate the grammar.

    KEY Open answers

Reading (page 14)

11. The reading task is based on R&W7. Candidates tend to find Part 7 difficult. It's important to train learners to read the whole

6

This is my family

text before starting to write the missing words, which is the purpose of the questions in ex. 11. Encourage them to read quickly without asking any questions about vocabulary at this stage.

KEY **1** Madrid, Spain **2** 8.30 **3** Valencia

12 Now focus attention on the missing words. Tell learners they need to look at the whole sentence and think about what kind of word is missing, a verb, a possessive adjective, a preposition? Learners should do this individually and then compare answers with a partner.

KEY **1** her **2** by **3** finishes/ends **4** After **5** do **6** At **7** Their **8** but **9** they **10** my

13 They should check their work again by answering the questions in ex. 13.
As a follow-up, you could ask learners to find an example of the possessive plural in the text (cousins' in the last line.)

KEY Open answers

Vocabulary (page 14)

14 Learners can do ex. 14 in pairs. They should write the number of the player in the box. During feedback, practise the pronunciation of the new words.

KEY A5 B1 C3 D1 E2 F4 G2

15 Read the example. Then you can do an example of someone in the class and get the learners to guess who it is. Learners then repeat the activity in pairs.

KEY Open answers

Listening (page 15)

(3) See recording script on page 47.

16 The listening focuses on L1. Before candidates listen they are given time to read the questions and look at the pictures. It's important to train learners to look at the pictures carefully and think about the words they will hear.

KEY Open answers

17 Play the recording twice. Learners can check their answers in pairs. Then play the recording a third time if necessary, or get learners to check their answers by reading the recording script and listening at the same time.

KEY **1** B **2** A **3** C

18 This activity should be done as a mingle, so learners have the opportunity to speak to as many people as possible. Before starting, elicit the questions learners need to ask. Drill the questions if necessary.
Learners talk to different people until most learners have completed the task.

During feedback, learners should give complete sentences, e.g. *Danny has three brothers.*

KEY Open answers

19 Talktime activities are designed to give an opportunity for extended speaking. Look at the example with the class and then get them to work in pairs.
Correct any grammar/pronunciation mistakes in class feedback. You may want to use able learners as a model.

KEY Open answers

Writing (page 15)

20 The writing task is based on R&W9. Candidates have to answer questions in an email instead of bullet points. Here there is a model answer with gaps to complete. Learners write the missing words in pairs.

KEY **1** His **2** has **3** my **4** have

21 They can write the email in class or for homework.

KEY Sample answer

Dear Jess,
My family isn't very big. I have two sisters but I don't have any brothers. In my family everyone has dark hair, except my dad. His hair is grey!
Love
Peter

▶▶▶ Internet Project ◀◀◀

Read about Craig and find out some information about
1 his family
2 what he eats for breakfast
3 what time he gets up

KEY **1** He has got a dad, mum and a sister.
2 He eats Rice Krispies and jam on toast for breakfast. He drinks a glass of milk.
3 He gets up at 7 o'clock.

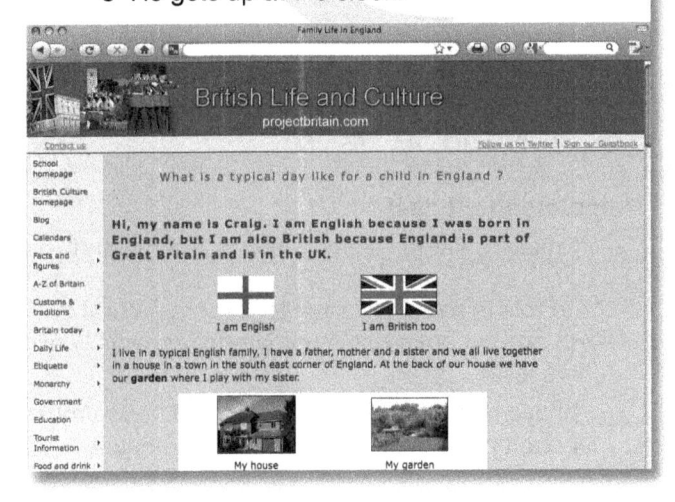

7

UNIT 3

KET topic	School and study
Vocabulary	Classroom objects; School subjects
Grammar	Modals of obligation: *have to/must*; *There is/are*; Adverbs of frequency
Reading	Describing education: **R&W4** Right/Wrong/Doesn't say
Writing	School: **R&W9** Email
Listening	Katie's new school: **L3** Multiple choice
Speaking	Describing education: **S1** Examiner's questions

Warmer (page 16)

1 The pictures show a girls' school in India and boys from Eton College in the UK, where this uniform is still worn. Check learners know the meaning of *uniform* before they discuss the questions in small groups or pairs.

KEY Open answers

Grammar (page 16)

2 Read the information about Nina and Robert. Write these examples on the board:
Nina has to wear a uniform.
Robert doesn't have to wear a uniform.
Then refer learners to the Grammar Bank and ask them to complete exercise 2 in pairs.
NB *have to* is used rather than *must* because we are talking about rules.
Feedback. Correct any mistakes. If further practice is needed, get learners to cover up exercise 2 and make sentences orally about Nina and Robert from the table.

KEY 1 doesn't have to 2 has to 3 doesn't have to 4 don't have to 5 have to

3 Learners write sentences individually. You could extend this task by getting learners to make sentences orally about the class using *we*, e.g. *We don't have to wear a uniform.*

KEY Open answers

4 Learners can do this in pairs. Don't pre-teach any vocabulary – encourage learners to guess.

KEY 1B 2F 3D 4A 5E 6C

Complete the Rules!
KEY 1 must, have to 2 don't have to 3 mustn't

5 Do this in pairs. NB *have to* is more natural in q3 and q5 but *must* is not wrong, especially at this level.

KEY 1 have to/must 2 doesn't have to 3 has to/must 4 don't have to 5 have to/must 6 mustn't

Vocabulary (page 17)

6 Learners can do this in pairs. Practise pronunciation in feedback.

KEY 1A 2E 3F 4D 5C 6H 7B 8G

7 Learners do this in pairs. There's no need to teach the grammar at this stage. NB B is not an acceptable answer for 1 because the question isn't asking for a number as a response.

KEY 1C 2B 3D 4E 5A 6F

8 Ask the class questions about things in your classroom. Use the same questions as ex. 7 and then add some others. NB *How many* is covered in Unit 6 so learners can just learn it as a phrase for now. Check they are using *there is/there are* accurately.

KEY Open answers

Reading (page 18)

9 Look at the picture of the school. Ask learners a few questions about it: Where do you think it is? Is it a big school? Is it a new school?
This is based on R&W4. Look at the example with the class. Explain what *Doesn't say* means. Then ask learners to read the first paragraph and find the text which gives the answer. It's a good idea to get them into the habit of underlining the key information in the text.

KEY 1B 2B 3A 4C 5C 6B 7A

10 Ask which subjects Manel studies. Then do ex. 10. Highlight the spelling and pronunciation of *languages* and *sport* as learners often have problems with these.

KEY Open answers

11 You could get learners to read the text again putting a tick or a cross where things in their school are the same or different to Manel's. Get learners to make sentences: *I have four hours of Science every week. My school is* new

8

Teaching & learning

and modern. There are four hundred students in my school.
Follow-up. Practise *there is/there are* with short answers: *Yes, there is/No there isn't*, etc. Ask questions about the learners' school(s), e.g. *Is there an art room in your school?*, *Yes, there is*. Do this in open class and then in pairs (but only if learners go to different schools – otherwise it's not very communicative).

KEY Open answers

Grammar (page 18)

12 Look at the diagram of adverbs of frequency in the Grammar Bank. Make some statements about yourself and ask the class to say if they are true or not.

KEY ... we usually **finish** at 3.35 p.m.
... study for the exams and **sometimes** I have a rest.

13 Drill a few examples of *How often do you...?* questions to develop a natural rhythm, before getting learners to ask and answer in pairs.

KEY Open answers

14 Learners take turns to ask the questions and write down at least one answer from each person in the group.
You can extend this task by getting learners to write true/false statements about themselves using adverbs of frequency. They read their sentences aloud and the class guesses if they are true/false.

KEY Open answers

Writing (page 19)

15 This is based on R&W9. Here learners have to answer three questions from a text. A model answer (with gaps) is provided here.

KEY **1** start **2** usually **3** of

16 Learners can write their own emails in class or for homework.

KEY Sample answer

> Dear Alex,
> My lessons start at 8.30. Lunch is at 1.30. I usually have a sandwich and some fruit. We can do basketball, hockey and tennis at my school. I like tennis best.
> Madeleine

Listening (page 19)

See recording script on page 47.

17 This is based on L3. In the actual test there are five questions plus an example. Give the class time to read through the questions before you play the recording.

KEY **1** C **2** A **3** B **4** A

18 Learners check their answers by reading the recording script. It's useful for learners to listen and read at the same time.

KEY Open answers

Speaking (page 19)

19 This is preparation for S1 where candidates have to answer some questions about their daily life.

KEY **1** What's, do **2** Are, them **3** Is, about

20 This practises extended speaking. In the speaking test candidates are asked one or two open questions which give an opportunity for a limited amount of extended speaking (perhaps three or four sentences).

▶▶▶ Internet Project ◀◀◀

This page describes a typical uniform in a British school. It also lists some advantages and disadvantages of wearing a school uniform. Read the page and answer the following questions.
1 Which reasons do you agree with for wearing/not wearing a school uniform?
2 Can you think of any other reasons?
3 Do you think it's a good idea for students in your school to wear a uniform?

EXAM BANK PP 20–21

R&W8
1 Saturday **2** 7.30p.m. **3** £3.50 **4** car **5** camera

R&W6
1 uniform **2** rucksack **3** dictionary **4** board **5** library

L2

See recording script on page 47.
1 E **2** D **3** F **4** A **5** C

S1
Open answers

UNIT 4

KET topic	Hobbies and leisure
Vocabulary	Leisure activities
Grammar	Present Continuous; *Wh* questions; Present Simple vs Present Continuous
Reading	Current activities: **R&W3** Matching; What do teenagers read?
Writing	Free time: **R&W9** Email
Listening	Music lessons: **L4** Gap-fill
Speaking	Expressing preferences; Hobbies

Warmer (page 22)

1 Learners discuss the answers. Elicit different kinds of music: *pop, reggae, rock, hip hop* are all on the KET wordlist. Further questions: *Are there any bands like this in your school?*, *Would you like to be in a band?*

KEY **1** drums, guitar, keyboard **2** rock music
3/4 Open answers

Vocabulary (page 22)

2 Check learners understand the meaning of *hobbies*, before they do the exercise in pairs.

KEY **1**F **2**A **3**G **4**E **5**B **6**H **7**D **8**C

3 Tell the class about the things you like/ don't like doing from the list in ex. 2 to provide a model. Learners make sentences orally in pairs. Then complete the rule in the box.
Extension task: Learners write three questions each to find out more about classmates' free time activities. For example, they could find out whether they like watching a particular TV programme or listening to a particular band.

KEY Open answers

Complete the Rules!
KEY infinitive

Grammar (page 23)

4 Look at the pictures and elicit the answers to the questions orally. Now get learners to look at the Grammar Bank and write the answers.

KEY **1** snowing **2** No, he isn't. He's playing the computer **3** No he isn't. He's laughing **4** No, they aren't. They're listening to music.

5/6 Learners do this in pairs.
Extension task. Choose 8 learners to each mime one of the activities in exercise 2. They should stand up or come to the front. Ask the rest of the class questions, e.g. *Is Luisa painting a picture?* The class responds: *No, she isn't. She's taking a photo.*

KEY Open answers

7 Do q1 as an example, before learners complete the ex. in pairs.

KEY **1** is having **2** are you making **3** Do you listen
4 I usually watch **5** is practising

Reading (page 23)

8 This is based on R&W3. Look at the example with the whole class. Explain they should make sure answers fit with both the sentence before and after each gap.
Learners complete the conversation individually and then compare answers in pairs.

KEY **1**B **2**H **3**G **4**F **5**A

Grammar (page 24)

9 Get learners to complete the questions in pairs. Then correct in open class.

KEY **1** Who **2** Where **3** What **4** Why **5** Which
6 When

10 Ask learners to try and put the questions in the correct order. You could do the first one as an example with the class. Then get them to check their answers by looking at the table in the Grammar Bank.
Extension task. Learners write three *Wh* questions to ask their partner about a free time activity, e.g. *When do you watch TV? What's your favourite programme? Why do you like it?* Monitor and correct any mistakes before learners take turns to ask/answer the questions.

KEY **1** What do you like doing in your free time?
2 Why do people like your music?
3 When does the band usually practise?

Complete the Rules!
KEY **1** where **2** what, which **3** when **4** who
5 why

10

Rock school

Reading (page 24)

11 This task is preparation for R&W4 but there's no *Doesn't say* option. Read through statements 1-6 with the class, checking everyone understands. Ask the class to say which ones they think are true.
KEY Open answers

12 Give learners a few minutes to read and put a tick or a cross next to each statement. They can compare answers with a partner.
KEY 1T 2T 3F 4T 5T 6F

13 Don't expect learners to reproduce the text accurately. If they find it difficult you can prompt them by giving the number, e.g. 23%. This kind of activity can be useful for developing fluency.
KEY Open answers

14 Learners say what is true for them, e.g. *I often read in my free time.* In pairs they can find out if they like/don't like the same writers.
Follow-up. If you have access to readers at this level, suggest that learners start to read stories in English or bring some to the class.
KEY Open answers

Listening (page 25)

(6) See recording script on page 47.

15 This is a lead-in practising listening for specific information.
KEY £40

16 Look at the notes for ex. 17 in detail with the class. Elicit the kind of information that's missing. Candidates are given time to do this in the test and it's important to train them how to use this time effectively.
KEY 1 word 2 number 3 word 4 number 5 word

17 Play the recording. Learners can check their answers with a partner before the second listening. If learners have problems understanding numbers/letters, you'll need to do some remedial work with them.
Feedback. Learners can check the recording script for their answers.
KEY 1 guitar 2 £10 3 Saturday 4 0777 312456 5 Crichton

Speaking (page 25)

18 This is a mingling activity. Before they start, elicit the questions learners need to ask. Learners should write the name of one person who does each of these things.
KEY Open answers

19 This is preparation for S1.
KEY Open answers

Writing (page 25)

20 This is practice for R&W9. To do well in the test candidates must answer all three questions in the email. The answer here does not say why she likes photography or how often she does it.
KEY 1 No. She doesn't answer the second or third questions. 2 No, it's only 22 words long – it's too short.

21 Learners can do this in class or for homework.
KEY Sample answer

Hi Beth,
My favourite hobby is playing the clarinet. I really like its sound and I like learning new music. I have lessons every Wednesday and also play in the school orchestra.
Fatma

▶▶▶ Internet Project ◀◀◀

This BBC site has some very short clips giving advice to young musicians. The language is authentic and some of the accents difficult but learners may find it interesting/motivating and should be able to access the task at a very basic level.

Choose one of the musicians and find out three facts about them.

UNIT 5

KET topic	Sport
Vocabulary	Sports; Verb-noun collocations
Grammar	Comparative & superlative adjectives; *Can/can't*; Adverbs of manner
Reading	Baseball: **R&W5** Multiple-choice cloze
Writing	Sport: **R&W9** Email
Listening	Sport: **L1** Multiple-choice pictures
Speaking	Asking about sport

Warmer (page 26)

1. Elicit *hockey* and *surfing*. Check learners understand the meaning of the adjectives. In pairs learners make sentences, e.g. *I think hockey is difficult.*
   - KEY Open answers

Vocabulary (page 26)

2. In pairs learners complete the names of the sports and match them to pictures A-J. Check the spelling and pronunciation.
   - KEY 1 tennis G 2 golf H 3 skiing E 4 cycling F 5 volleyball J 6 sailing I 7 climbing A 8 skating B 9 fishing C 10 basketball D

3. Ask learners if they *play climbing* or *go climbing*. Learners write the correct letter for each sport in the correct box.
   - KEY Play: tennis, golf, volleyball, basketball
         Go: skiing, cycling, sailing, climbing, skating, fishing

4. Do a few examples with the class. Check the pronunciation of the adjectives before learners do the task in pairs.
   - KEY Open answers

Grammar (page 27)

5. Look at the sentences together. Ask learners if they agree. Translate if necessary. Explain that *sailing isn't as popular as surfing* means the same as *surfing is more popular than sailing.*
   - KEY Open answers

Complete the Rules!
Learners read the information in the Grammar Bank and decide if rules 1-3 are correct.
   - KEY Sentence 3 is correct.

6. Do the first sentence as an example. Learners complete the rest using the Grammar Bank to help them.

Feedback. Go through the answers. If learners need further practice, write all the adjectives from this unit on the board and elicit the comparative and superlative forms. They can also do the exercises in the Grammar Bank.
Extension task. Learners write comparative and superlative sentences about their favourite sports/teams, e.g. *Inter is the best team in Italy at the moment.*
   - KEY 1 more dangerous 2 stronger 3 easier 4 as popular 5 best 6 fastest

Reading (page 27)

7. This task is based on R&W5. Ask learners if they play/watch baseball. What do they think of it? Learners tick the countries they think play women's baseball before they read.
   Learners skim the text to find out where women's baseball is played. It's important to train learners to read the whole text before trying to fill the gaps.
   - KEY The USA, Canada, Japan, India, Korea, Iran

8. In the actual test only one comparative or superlative form might be targeted and each option would only appear once. Emphasise the importance of reading the whole sentence carefully before choosing the correct option. Learners can do this individually and then check their answers with a partner.
   Follow-on: discuss whether baseball is popular in your country for girls and boys.
   - KEY 1A 2B 3B 4A 5C 6B

Listening (page 28)

(7) See recording script on page 48.

9. This is based on L1. This prediction task helps prepare learners for the listening. In the actual test candidates are given time to study the questions and pictures, and learners should use this time to focus on the words they are likely to hear.
   Go through the other questions and pictures

12

Can you surf?

with the class, identifying the vocabulary, numbers and times in the pictures.

KEY football, favourite, hockey, skiing, enjoy, fun

10 Learners listen and then check their answers with a partner before the second listening.

KEY 1B 2A 3B 4B

11 Play the recording again while learners read the script.

Grammar (page 29)

12 To demonstrate the task, read the sentences aloud and tell the class which are true for you. Write 'very well, well, quite well, not at all' on the board in descending order to clarify the meaning. Learners do the task in pairs. Feedback. Learners may be embarrassed to admit to being very good at tennis or not being able to ride a bike, so avoid whole class feedback here.

KEY Open answers

13 Prompt learners to ask you questions. *Can you...?* Answer them using quite well, etc. Drill the questions and then get learners to ask/answer in pairs.
Learners look at the Grammar Bank to complete the rules.
Extension task. Learners write sentences about the sports they can/can't do.

KEY Open answers

Complete the Rules!

KEY 1 doesn't change 2 without 3 doesn't use

Speaking (page 29)

14 This is preparation for S2 where learners have to form questions from prompts. Elicit the full questions and drill.

KEY Open answers

15 Learners take turns to ask and answer. Feedback. Find out which sports are the most popular or about any unusual sports played by learners.

KEY Open answers

16 This is preparation for S1 where learners do a very short extended speaking task (four or five sentences max). They are not expected to speak for one minute but it's good for building fluency and also to stretch the strongest learners.

KEY Open answers

Writing (page 29)

17 This is based on R&W9. Here learners evaluate a sample answer. In order to gain good marks in this part of the test, learners are not expected to produce error free emails. But unless good spelling is encouraged at this stage, learners will get into bad habits. Learners discuss the questions in pairs. They should find and correct the spelling errors. There's also a punctuation error.

KEY 1 Yes 2 Yes – 35 words 3 5 – tenis, hes, beter, favourit, ski

18 Learners can do this in class or for homework. Follow-on. Get learners to peer correct each others' work using questions 1-3 in ex. 17.

KEY Sample answer

> Dear Joe,
> I like rugby, but I'm not very good at it. I am very good at athletics and take part in competitions. Yes, I can swim, I go every Sunday with my Dad.
> Later,
> David

▶▶▶ Internet Project ◀◀◀

This is a guide to Olympic cyclist's Chris Hoy's racing bike. Chris Hoy won three gold medals for Great Britain at the 2008 Olympic Games in Beijing. Find three differences between a normal bike and an Olympic racing bike.

KEY From: lighter frame, no gears, different handlebars and wheels.

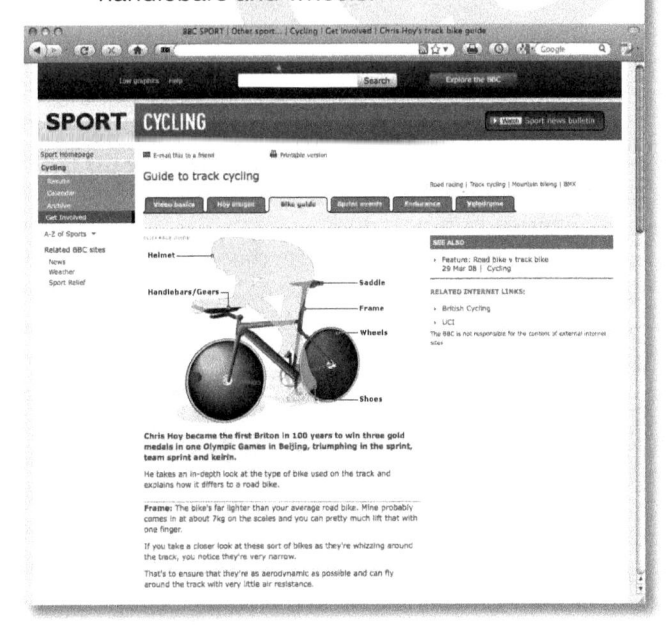

UNIT 6

KET topics	Food and drink; Social interaction
Vocabulary	Food & drink
Grammar	Countable & uncountable nouns; *have/has got; how much/how many?*
Reading	School meals: **R&W4** Right/Wrong/Doesn't say
Writing	Expressing preferences: **R&W9** Email
Listening	Choosing a restaurant: **L2** Matching
Speaking	Ordering meals

Warmer (page 30)

1 Learners look at the picture and discuss the questions in pairs.

KEY Open answers

Reading (page 30)

2 Learners scan the text to find food words. TWrite a list of the food words on the board and explain the meaning if necessary. Drill the pronunciation of *vegetables*. Learners often have problems getting the stress on the first syllable.

KEY lunch, dish, menu, fish, lemon sauce, meal, home-cooked meal, healthy meal, rice, meat, eggs, vegetables

3 Discuss as a whole class and compare with school meals in your country.

KEY Open answers

4 This is based on R&W4. In the actual test there is usually only one text. Go through the example with the class. Tell them to underline the answers in the text. Check learners understand statements 1-6, before they do the task individually. Learners then check their answers with a partner.
Remind learners to read as much as they can.

KEY 1A 2C 3A 4A 5A 6B

Grammar (page 31)

5 Discuss this question as a whole class. Explain *countable* and *uncountable*. If you can count it, it's countable, e.g. *one egg, two eggs*, etc. If you can't count it, and it doesn't have a plural form, it's uncountable. You can't say *one rice, two rices*. NB some words can be both, e.g. *coffee* can be countable if it refers to cups of coffee, e.g. *We'd like three coffees please.*

KEY Uncountable: rice, meat
Countable: eggs, vegetables

6 Use flashcards to check/teach the meaning and practise the pronunciation of these words. Learners work in pairs to complete the table. Elicit some more food words from KET wordlist (see p. 102) using food flashcards. Learners then decide if they are countable/uncountable.

KEY Countable: orange, burger, sausage, biscuit
Uncountable: pasta, sugar, coffee, water

Complete the Rules!
Learners read the information in the Grammar Bank to complete the rules.

KEY 1 a 2 some 3 any

7 Learners do the exercise in pairs and use the Grammar Bank to check their answers.
Ask if they think Sarah's packed lunch is healthy. Find out what learners put in their packed lunches if they have them.

KEY 1 an 2 a 3 some 4 any 5 some 6 any

8 Explain that *How many* is used with countables and *How much* is used with uncountables. Check learners know the meaning of *sweets* and *fizzy*. Drill the questions paying attention to stress and intonation.

KEY 1 How many 2 How much 3 How much
4 How many 5 How much

9 Demonstrate the task by getting learners to ask you the questions.
Learners practise in pairs. They could do this as a mingling task to vary the interaction.

KEY Open answers

Vocabulary (page 32)

10 Learners can do the matching in pairs. Check the answers and practise saying the phrases naturally. Highlight the linking between the words, e.g. *cup* and *of* so that it sounds like *a cup of tea.*

KEY 1D 2E 3F 4B 5A 6C

A piece of cake

11 Learners answer the questions in pairs. You can elicit different types of cake/soup.

KEY **1** chocolate **2** vegetable **3** butter **4** open answer

12 Do the first one as an example. Then learners can work individually and check their answers in pairs.
Extension activity. Learners can play a variation of 'I went to the supermarket and I bought...' Each learner has to repeat what the last person said and add an item of their own, e.g. Student A: *For lunch I usually have a ham sandwich.* Student B: *For lunch I usually have a ham sandwich and an apple.* And so on around the class.

KEY **1** cheese **2** jam **3** coffee **4** ice cream **5** orange juice **6** fruit

Writing (page 32)

13 This is based on R&W9. Here learners are given two sample answers to evaluate. Learners should read all three emails and decide in pairs which is a better answer.

KEY B is a better answer because it is more fluent and uses linking words such as *so*. The language is more sophisticated and the length is correct at 34 words.

14 Learners can write their email in class or for homework.
Follow-on. Get learners to evaluate each others' work.

KEY Sample answer

> Dear Imran,
> I finish school at 2.30 so I can come to your house at 3 o'clock. I'd like to go to the pool if it's sunny. I like most food except cheese.

Listening (page 33)

(8) See recording script on page 48.

15 This is preparation for the matching task which is based on L2.

KEY Pizza

16 Before they listen, learners should look at the questions and options. Explain that they hear the names of the restaurants in order. This makes it easier to follow the conversation. Check learners understand the meaning of *friendly waiters*.
Learners listen and then check their answers with a partner before listening again.

KEY **1**B **2**F **3**E **4**A **5**G

17 Learners can listen and read at the same time.

KEY **1** And it doesn't cost much. **2** They have tables under the trees. It's lovely in summer. **3** But I can't hear what anyone is saying in there. It's so noisy. **4** That's a good place for large groups. They have lots of room. **5** That opens this week.

Speaking (page 33)

18 You could get learners to ask you the questions and give some model answers, before they take turns to ask and answer in pairs.

KEY Open answers

19 Go through the menu and explain any new words. NB *dessert* is sometimes used on menus instead of *puddings*. Learners complete the conversation. Then check it in open class. Drill the sentences focusing on natural rhythm and intonation.

KEY **1** a **2** some **3** a **4** any **5** any **6** some

20-21 Learners role play the conversation in groups of three. Depending on time and space available you could set the classroom up as a restaurant.

KEY Open answers

Internet Project

Take this healthy eating quiz. What score do you get?

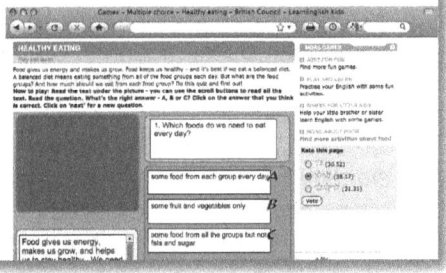

EXAM BANK PP 34-35

R&W3
1C 2A 3A 4B 5B

R&W9
Sample answer

> Dear Patrick,
> On Saturdays I go swimming. On Sundays I play football. I do my homework in the afternoon. I don't watch a lot of TV because I don't have much time.
> Simon

L4

(9) See recording script on page 48.
1 school bus **2** 15 October **3** 2.30 p.m. **4** 15 **5** 454 6610

S2
Open answers

15

UNIT 7

KET topics	Transport; Travel and holidays
Vocabulary	Holiday words and activities; Transport
Grammar	Past Simple; Prepositions of place
Reading	Giving information about places
Writing	Holidays: **R&W9** Postcard
Listening	Talking about past events: **L3** Multiple choice
Speaking	Asking for and giving travel information

Warmer (page 36)

1   Ask learners where they usually go on holiday. Look at the photos. Ask learners to say which country each place is in. Learners discuss the questions briefly in pairs. They don't need to describe activities or places in any detail.

KEY   Open answers

Vocabulary (page 36)

2   Learners match the words and pictures. Encourage them to guess if they're not sure.

KEY   **1** pyramid, sand, tour guide, desert   **2** lake, forest, campsite, mountain & tent   **3** mountain, beach, sand & sea   **4** snowman

3   Do this as a whole class activity. Explain *sightseeing*, *theme parks* and *adventures* by giving some well-known examples from your country. In pairs learners brainstorm at least one more activity for each picture, e.g. 1. go sailing on the River Nile, ride a camel 2. go fishing, 3. Go swimming, 4. Go skiing, snowboarding, etc.

KEY   **1** go sightseeing, have adventures   **2** do sports, have adventures   **3** do sports, go to theme parks, go to the beach, read, go shopping   **4** do sports, have adventures

4   Learners discuss their favourite holiday activities. Extension task: learners make a chart of the most visited holiday destinations in the class.

KEY   Open answers

Reading (page 37)

5   This is preparation for R&W4 but there isn't a 'Doesn't say' option here. This is a gist-reading activity to encourage learners to read for the main idea. It may be worth setting a time limit of about two minutes to try and improve learners' reading speed.

KEY   Picture 3

6   Learners can discuss this in pairs.

KEY   Kate likes going shopping.

7   Learners do the task individually and then check their answers with a partner. Ask learners if they would like to go to Salou.

KEY   **1**B **2**A **3**A **4**B **5**B **6**B

Grammar (page 37)

8   Look at the Past Simple examples with the class. Ask which verbs they think are regular and which one is irregular. Go through the formation of regular past tense endings of *stay*, *travel*, *study* on the board.

KEY   went (go). We form the past of regular verbs by adding -ed to the infinitive.

9   Look at the verbs in the box. Ask which ones are regular. Elicit the irregular endings. If the class doesn't know them, refer to the list of irregular verb forms on p. 111. Look at the picture of the elephant. Ask learners where they think this is. Ask if anyone would like to ride an elephant. Pre-teach *jungle*, *waterfall*, *river*, *monkey*. Learners read Oliver's postcard quickly and then complete it. Explain that they only need positive forms. Feedback: go through the answers. Drill the pronunciation of *wanted*, *visited*, *rode*, *were*.

KEY   **1** visited **2** went **3** was **4** rode **5** had **6** loved **7** wanted **8** were

10   Look at the verbs in the box. Ask which ones are regular/irregular. Elicit the Past Simple forms (positive and negative). Demonstrate the activity by telling the class what you did/didn't do yesterday. Learners practise in pairs. They can do this orally.
Extension task. Learners write sentences about their last holiday using some of the verbs from ex. 9 and 10.

KEY   Open answers

16

Out and about

Vocabulary (page 38)

11 Point out that *bike* is often used instead of *bicycle* and that *plane* is short for *aeroplane*. Explain that a *ship* is big boat and *boat* can be used for smaller vessels.

KEY 1A 2E 3B 4D 5C 6F 7H 8G

12 This is preparation for R&W6 where candidates read definitions and have to spell the word correctly. Learners may find some of the words challenging but they are all on the KET wordlist. You may want to pre-teach *wheel, machine, factory, sky.*

KEY 1D 2B 3H 4G 5A 6F 7C 8E

Speaking (page 38)

13 Do the first question as an example. Remind the class that, as in the Present Simple, to make questions with all verbs (apart from the verb 'be'), they must use the auxiliary *do*, i.e. *did*. Learners continue in pairs. Before learners ask/answer the questions in pairs, check they are correct. Drill, focusing on natural rhythm and intonation. Learners practise in pairs or they can mingle.

KEY 1 Where did you go on holiday last year?
2 Where did you stay? 3 How did you travel there? 4 What did you do there?

14 This is preparation for S1 where candidates have an opportunity for extended speaking (four or five sentences). They are not expected to speak for one minute but this is a chance to challenge stronger learners.

KEY Open answers

15 Look at the map with the class and identify the various locations. Establish where the beach is. Check learners understand the words in the box. Draw simple diagrams on the board to clarify, or use the map. Learners complete the sentences in pairs.

KEY 1 in the middle of the park. 2 in front of the beach. 3 behind the station. 4 between the school and the hospital. 5 next to the car park.

16 Demonstrate the activity with a strong learner. Drill the question. Then practise in open pairs. Learners practise again in closed pairs.

KEY Open answers

17 Ask learners to think about where their school/house is. Ask questions referring to local landmarks. *Is your house near... park? Is your school in front of... station?*

KEY Open answers

Listening (page 39)

(10) See recording script on page 48.

18 This is preparation for L3. This exercise trains learners to read the questions carefully before they listen and to think about the content of what they will hear. Candidates are given time to do this in the actual test. This task is designed to show that options A, B and C are all mentioned in the text – but just because they hear one of the options, doesn't mean it's the answer.

KEY Open answers

19 Learners listen to confirm their predictions for ex. 18. They discuss the answers to the multiple-choice questions and then listen again.

KEY 1B 2B 3C 4C 5A

20 Ask learners to try and identify the reasons for any mistakes.

21 This task is preparation for R&W9 where candidates are sometimes asked to write a postcard. Learners have to fill in the missing verbs in the model answer, discriminating between the Present and Past Simple.

KEY 1 is 2 has 3 went 4 visited 5 had

22 Learners write their postcard in class or for homework.

KEY Sample answers

> Dear Aunt Julia,
> We are in a pretty hotel in the centre. It has a lovely garden where we can have breakfast. Yesterday we went to the top of the Eiffel Tower – what wonderful views.
> Love,
> Sarah

▶▶▶ Internet Project ◀◀◀

Click on the map on Morocco, Egypt, Kenya or Tanzania. Find three things you can do on holiday there.

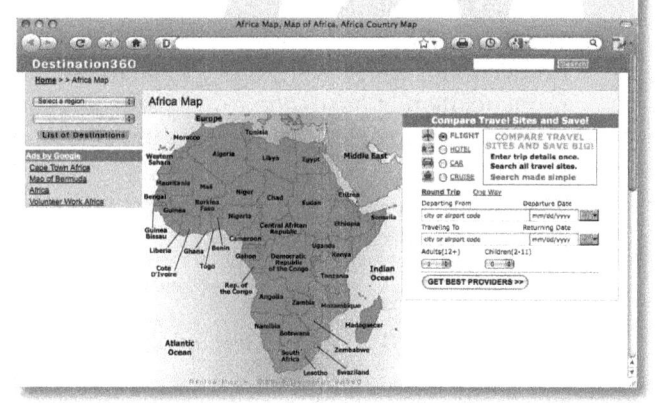

UNIT 8

KET topics	Health, medicine and exercise
Vocabulary	Parts of the body; Health; Understanding simple signs
Grammar	*Should/shouldn't*; Past Continuous: simple narratives
Reading	Understanding narratives
Writing	Giving advice and sympathising: **R&W9** Email
Listening	Safety rules: **L5** Gap-fill
Speaking	Giving warnings and stating prohibitions

Warmer (page 40)

1 Look at the picture. Ask learners to describe what the players are doing. Write verb prompts on the board to help them: *run, kick, sit down, lie down, shout.* Ask if this is a good game of football.

KEY Open answers

Vocabulary (page 40)

2 Check learners understand 'parts of the body'. They may find this challenging so don't leave them in pairs too long.

KEY **1** back **2** hand **3** foot **4** eye **5** arm **6** leg **7** ear **8** head

3 Teach *hurt, broken, pain, cut*. Remind the class that *he's got = he has got* which means the same as *has*.
Learners complete the sentences individually. Then they read their sentences aloud in random order to their partner who points to the correct player.

KEY **1** foot **2** leg **3** back **4** head **5** ear **6** arm **7** eye **8** hand

Grammar (page 41)

4 Explain that *should/ shouldn't* is used when you want to help someone with a problem. Elicit the answer to question 1.
Learners complete the sentences. They can use the Grammar Bank to help them.
Feedback. Check the answers and then ask if Petra's mum believes she's ill. Practise the pronunciation of *headache*.
Learners complete the rules using the Grammar Bank.

KEY **1** shouldn't **2** should **3** shouldn't **4** shouldn't **5** shouldn't **6** should

Complete the Rules!

KEY **1** modal **2** *to* **3** should **4** shouldn't

5 Check learners understand *mobile phone, toothache, ill*. In pairs they think of suggestions using *should/shouldn't*. Feedback. Select some good learner responses to write on the board and some containing errors for the class to correct.

KEY *Suggested answers:* **1** You should do it again.
2 You should ask the shop to repair it.
3 You should go to the dentist.
4 You should take it to the vet.

Writing (page 41)

6 This task is preparation for R&W9. Tell learners to make sure they answer the three questions.

KEY Sample answer

> Dear Luke,
> Sorry you are ill. Why don't you try to go to sleep and then do your homework later? Yes, I'm free tomorrow and you can come to my house after school if you like.
> From
> Matt

7 Learners work in pairs to find the mistakes.

KEY I am sorry you can't ~~to~~ come to my house.
I think you shouldn't **do** your homework.
You should ~~to~~ sleep.

Vocabulary (page 41)

8 Look at the example with the class. Learners use the model to talk about the other signs.

KEY **2** No dogs, for example in shops or restaurants, etc. You can't take dogs in these places because dogs are not always hygienic. **3** No running, possibly in places where running could be dangerous, i.e. at the side of a swimming pool. **4** No swimming could be at the beach where it might be dangerous to swim due to water pollution or possible shark attacks, for example. **5** No diving, often found in a

Be careful!

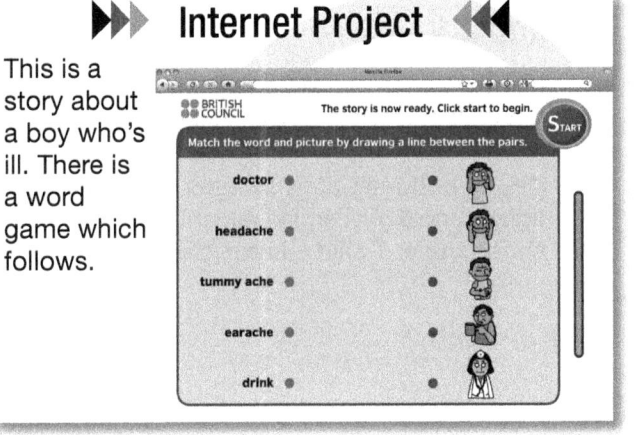

swimming pool where the water isn't deep enough. **6** No mobile phone, for example, in a library where there is supposed to be silence.

Reading (page 42)

9 Ask the class if they like barbecues. Do they often have them at home? What do they cook on the barbecue?
Tell the class to read the story and put the pictures in order. There may be some unfamiliar words but these should not present comprehension problems as learners have pictures to support them. Learners compare the order of the pictures. Elicit the correct order and write it on the board.

KEY **1**E **2**C **3**B **4**A **5**G **6**H **7**D **8**F

10 In pairs learners discuss the questions.
KEY **1** four **2** chicken **3** because the shoe hit her in the eye

Grammar (page 42)

11 Write *While Dan's dad was using a sharp knife to cut the sausages, he cut his finger.* on the board. Check learners understand the meaning. Then highlight the use of the Past Continuous. Learners underline examples of Past Simple and Past Continuous in the text. They could use different colours for this.
KEY Past Simple: was, decided, was, cut, didn't need, phoned, didn't see, thought, took, was, was, threw, didn't hit, hit, had, put, ate, decided, had, wasn't, said, wanted
Past Continuous: was using, was cooking, was talking, was lying, was hurting,

12 Do the first sentence with the class. Learners do the rest in pairs using the Grammar Bank to help them.
KEY **1** was cleaning, fell **2** didn't go, wasn't feeling **3** broke, were skiing **4** were swimming, saw **5** was working, met **6** didn't go, was raining

13 This activity is good for building fluency. Learners can take turns in pairs to describe the pictures in order. You could write key words/phrases on the board to help them.
KEY Open answers

Listening (page 43)

🎧 (11) **See recording script on page 48.**

14 This is preparation for L4. Check learners understand *skateboard park* and the words in the box. This is a gist listening task to encourage learners to think about the purpose of the text.
KEY Teenage skateboarders

15 This is a scanning task to focus learners on numbers. Part 4 tasks usually contain at least two numbers.
KEY 9, 7, 10 p.m., 12-18, £1.50

16-18 Get learners to identify whether they need to write a number (a price? a date? a time?) or another kind of word. See if learners can write the missing information before they listen again.
After learners have completed the task, find out if any of them go to skate parks. Are the rules similar to this one?
KEY **1** 7 **2** 12-18 **3** drinks **4** music **5** 1.50

Speaking (page 43)

19 You could demonstrate the task by describing the rules at a pool/cinema/park you go to.
KEY Open answers

20 Ask learners to think of some ideas for a minute and then do this as a whole class activity.
KEY Open answers

21 Explain the phrase *scaredy cat* – used to describe someone who is afraid of everything. You may need to pre-teach *cry, angry, don't mind*. Learners complete the questionnaire individually.
When filling in the questionnaire for their partner, it isn't necessary for them to form questions e.g. *Do you cry...?* or *Would you like...?*
KEY Open answers

22 Do this as a whole class activity. NB Some boys may be reluctant to admit to crying and if you sense the class feels uncomfortable about discussing this you can move on to the next activity.
KEY Open answers

23 Tell the class about anything you are afraid of.
KEY Open answers

▶▶▶ **Internet Project** ◀◀◀

This is a story about a boy who's ill. There is a word game which follows.

19

UNIT 9

KET topic	Clothes
Vocabulary	Colours; Items of clothing; Materials
Grammar	Order of adjectives: describing simple objects; *Need*: expressing needs
Reading	Colour can change the way you think: **R&W5** Multiple-choice cloze
Writing	Giving and responding to invitations: **R&W9** Email
Listening	Buying things; Paying compliments: **L3** Multiple choice
Speaking	Buying things

Warmer (page 44)

1 Learners answer the questions in pairs. Feedback. Identify the colours in the picture. Ask if learners like the picture.

KEY **1** dark blue, light blue, dark green, light green, yellow, red, pink, orange, brown, grey
2-4 Open answers

Reading (page 44)

2 This is preparation for R&W5. This task trains learners to read the whole text before attempting to fill the gaps. Learners read the text quickly. Don't answer any vocabulary questions at this stage.

KEY **1** People living in hot countries. **2** People living in cold countries. **3** Yellow is a warm colour which makes you feel happier and relaxed. **4** Open answers

3 Look at the example with the class. Emphasise the importance of reading the whole sentence to look for clues about tense or agreement. Learners work individually and then compare answers in pairs.

KEY **1**B **2**A **3**B **4**C **5**A **6**B **7**B **8**A

4 Talk about the colours people wear in your country.

KEY Open answers

Vocabulary (page 45)

5 Learners work in pairs to label the pictures. Feedback. Practise the pronunciation especially *skirt, shirt, trousers*.

KEY (Top to bottom) *Cathy:* sweater, coat, skirt, tights, boots. *Oscar:* jacket, shirt, tie, trousers, shoes. *Jude:* T-shirt, shorts, trainers.

6 Teach the words for the materials and then elicit sentences.

KEY *Suggested answers:* **Cathy** is wearing a leather jacket, a wool skirt and leather boots. **Jude** is wearing a cotton T-shirt and cotton shorts.

7 Do this in pairs or as a whole class.

KEY **1**D **2**C **3**B **4**A

Grammar (page 45)

8 Explain that in English adjectives have to go in a particular order. Look at the table in the Grammar Bank and go through the example.
Learners work in pairs. Tell them to use the Grammar Bank to help them.

KEY **1** expensive black leather **2** dirty old blue
3 nice warm wool(len) purple **4** smart dark wool(len) **5** pretty new summer

9 Learners can write sentences describing the clothes in the pictures.

KEY *Suggested answers:* **Cathy** is wearing a purple leather coat, a pink wool skirt and beige leather boots. **Jude** is wearing a red cotton T-shirt and light blue cotton shorts.

10 Learners describe their clothes to their partner. If they're wearing school uniform they can talk about what they like wearing at the weekend.

KEY Open answers

Listening (page 46)

(12) See recording script on page 49.

11 This is a gist listening activity to prepare for the L3 multiple-choice task. It's important for learners to listen to the whole conversation, which is quite short. It's easy for candidates to get stuck on a question and miss the rest of the conversation.

KEY No, she doesn't.

I need a hat!

12-13 In pairs learners try to answer questions 1-5. Learners then listen again and answer the questions.

KEY **1**C **2**C **3**B **4**A **5**A

14-15 Play the recording again while learners read the script. You could play the sentences from ex. 14 again and pause for learners to repeat.

KEY **1** looking for **2** much **3** quite **4** it on **5** feels

Speaking (page 46)

16 Learners can either practise the role plays in pairs or you can set up two or three shops in the classroom, dividing the accessories between them. Feedback. You could ask some students to act out their role play in front of the class. Highlight any errors from the class as a whole with target language.

KEY Open answers

17 Elicit the questions to check for accuracy before learners ask and answer in pairs.

KEY Open answers

18 This is an opportunity for extended speaking. Candidates are not expected to speak for one minute in the actual test but in S1 there is a short 'long turn' where candidates produce four or five sentences.

KEY Open answers

Grammar (page 47)

19 Ask a few concept questions to clarify the meaning of *need*, e.g. *What do you need to wear to play football? What do you need if you want to buy something? What do you need to do if you are tired?* Look at the table in the Grammar Bank with the class. Point out that there are two forms of the negative *don't need to* and *needn't*. Learners often make mistakes by putting *needn't to*, so highlight this. Learners complete the exercise using the Grammar Bank to help them. Feedback. Correct any errors.

KEY **1** need **2** do, need **3** Do, need **4** don't need **5** doesn't need **6** needs **7** need **8** Does, need

20 Check learners understand *pack* and *suitcase*. Learners then decide in pairs what Jessica needs/doesn't need to pack.

KEY *Suggested answers:* **1** She needs to take the dress but she doesn't need to take her schools skirt. **2** She needs to take her hat, her jeans and her leather jacket but she doesn't need to take her shorts. **3** She needs to take her shorts but she doesn't need to take her hat.

21 Learners can do this orally or as a written exercise.

KEY Open answers

22 This is preparation for R&W9. Learners write emails individually.

KEY Sample answer

> Dear Alex,
> Yes, I'd like to go too. I'm free on Saturday afternoon. Let's meet at 3.30 at the bus stop. I need to buy a dress for a party so we can look for that.
> See you on Saturday,
> Louise

23 Learners should be able to identify if their partner has answered all the questions and written the right amount of words but they may find evaluating spelling/grammar mistakes harder. The main focus in the test is on communication not accuracy so this is of secondary importance. However, it's good to get learners to proofread their work.

KEY Open answers

▶▶▶ Internet Project ◀◀◀

This game revises key clothes vocabulary from the unit.

EXAM BANK *pp 48-49*

R&W1
1A **2**H **3**D **4**F **5**E

R&W9
Sample answer

> I have the flu and am in bed. Please don't come today, but can you come tomorrow afternoon? Can you bring a list of all the homework?
> Ellie

L1

(13) See recording script on page 49.
1A **2**B **3**C

S1
Open answers

UNIT 10

KET topic	Entertainment and media
Vocabulary	Verb-noun collocations; Entertainment; Television programmes
Grammar	Present Continuous: future arrangements; *May*
Reading	Are you a TV addict?
Writing	Responding to invitations: **R&W9** Email
Listening	Talking about future plans: **L2** Matching
Speaking	Plans for the weekend

Warmer (page 50)

1 During feedback you could elicit the names of TV programmes and/or some adjectives, e.g. *I think they're watching a funny/scary film.* NB *scary* would be appropriate here although it isn't on the KET wordlist.

KEY Open answers

Vocabulary (page 50)

2 Do this as a whole class activity, giving help with new any new words, e.g. *click*, *link*. Check learners understand the phrasal verbs *stay in* and *go out*.

KEY **1** in, to, out **2** at, on

3 This exercise introduces some common verb-noun collocations or fixed phrases, (although *visit a museum* strictly speaking, isn't a fixed phrase). You may need to pre-teach *chat online*, *sleepover*, before learners complete the task in pairs. You could extend the task by asking learners about their leisure time activities, e.g. *Do you always have a party to celebrate your birthday?*

KEY **1** having **2** stay **3** visited **4** make **5** had **6** making

Reading (page 51)

4 Teach the words for TV programmes by eliciting the names of well-known TV programmes in your country. The words here are taken from the KET wordlist but with an able class you could add one or two more which aren't on the list; e.g. *comedy*, *soap opera*. Learners find out how often their partner watches these kinds of TV show. Then ask a few learners to report back to the class.

KEY Open answers

5 Pre-teach *addict* and *addicted* (not on KET wordlist but the concept is easily accessible). Then get learners to complete the quiz individually and add up their scores. They then read the advice for their score.

KEY Open answers

6-7 Find out how many TV addicts there are in the class and follow this with a class discussion. *Is the advice good? Do they agree they have a problem with TV?* If there are no TV addicts in the class, ask if they know anyone who is.

KEY Open answers

Grammar (page 52)

8 Look at the information about the school trip and answer the questions in open class. Ask, *Is Georgia in London now or is she going in the future?* to make the concept clear. Remind learners the Present Continuous also describes things that are happening now.
Get learners to make sentences. *At 12 o'clock on Thursday, Georgia is visiting the Science Museum.* NB the photo is of The Natural History Museum in London.
Ask questions. *Is Georgia having lunch in the hotel on Thursday?* The class responds, *No, she's having lunch at the museum.*

KEY **1** She's having lunch at the museum. **2** She's visiting Shakespeare's Globe Theatre. **3** She's going shopping at 4 o'clock on Thursday.

9 Using the Grammar Bank, learners write five questions to ask their partner. They can ask/answer with books closed from memory to make it more challenging.

KEY Open answers

10 Find out if learners would like to visit, or have visited London. Talk about the school trips that they do.

KEY Open answers

11 Tell the class some things you may do tomorrow or at the weekend, e.g. *I may play tennis at the weekend.* Explain that this is a possibility not a plan.

What's on?

Ask learners to read the information in the Grammar Bank and then correct the mistakes in pairs. Learners also complete the rules.

KEY 1 delete the *to* after *may*   2 delete *don't* and add *not* after *may*   3 replace *goes* with *go*.

Complete the Rules!

KEY 1 are certain about   2 *unsure*

12 You can extend this task by getting learners to write negative/ positive sentences using the Present Continuous and *may* about their plans after school/ tomorrow/ the summer holidays.

KEY 1 am playing   2 may become   3 aren't going   4 may go   5 Are you staying   6 isn't meeting   7 Is Patrick having   8 may not go

Listening (page 53)

(14) See recording script on page 49.

13 This is preparation for L2. Get the class to look at the options carefully before they listen.

KEY 1F   2H   3B   4A   5G

14 After the second listening, get learners to correct their answers by looking at the recording script. They should also look for examples of the Present Continuous. Elicit phrases for inviting and suggesting from the script; *Would you like to ...? Shall we..?*

KEY You're coming, I'm bringing, Dad's taking, He isn't having, bands are playing, grandma's having

Speaking (page 53)

15 Tell learners to write *party* or *sleepover*, etc. in the diaries. They don't need to write the verb. Demonstrate with a strong student. Practise *Yes, I'd love to / Sorry, I can't*.

KEY Open answers

16-17 Tell the learners your plans for the weekend/ summer holidays, etc. Learners then work in pairs. Feedback. Get a few learners to report back. Encourage them to give full answers, e.g. *Eric's going to the beach this summer but I'm staying at home. We're both doing our Science homework this evening.*

KEY Open answers

Writing (page 53)

18-19 Elicit some phrases learners could use in the email, e.g. *Thank you very much for the invitation. I'm sorry I can't go to your house tomorrow. I have to go to the dentist. What about next Friday instead?* Write these on the board.

Learners write their emails in class or for homework. Get them to proofread their work and to check the number of words.

KEY Sample answer

> Dear Tommy,
> Thank you very much for inviting me to your house tomorrow. I'm afraid I can't come because I have to go to the dentist. Are you free on Friday? Can I come then?
> Laura

▶▶▶ Internet Project ◀◀◀

Learners go to the home page of this site which gives information about new films.

Decide which new film you would most like to see.

Answer these questions:

1 Who is the director?
2 Who are the main actors?
3 What is it about?

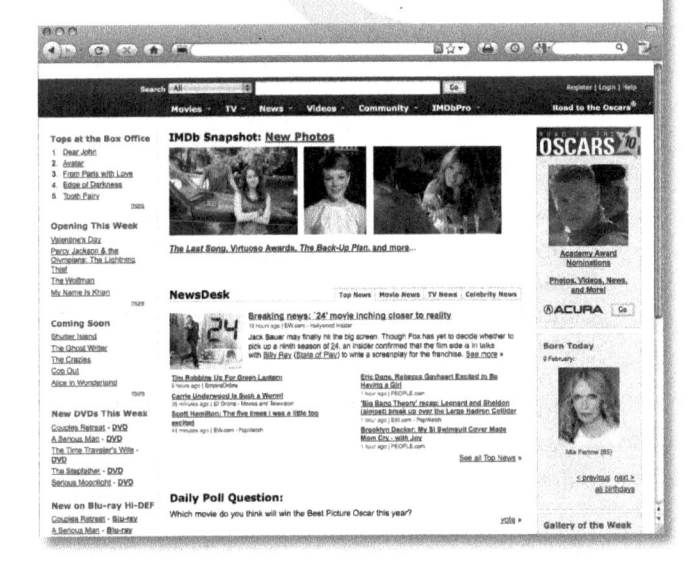

UNIT 11

KET topics	House and home
Vocabulary	Furniture; Rooms in the house
Grammar	Present Perfect with *for* and *since*
Reading	Zoe's bedroom
Writing	Describing accommodation: **R&W9** Email
Listening	A guided tour: **L5** Gap-fill
Speaking	Your perfect house

Warmer (page 54)

1 Look at the pictures. Ask which one is messy/tidy. Learners discuss the questions in pairs. You may want to find some other aids: flashcards of furniture, rooms in the house. Pictures of teenagers' bedrooms, etc.

KEY Open answers

Vocabulary (page 54)

2 Learners work in pairs to complete the words. If learners don't know any of the words, hold up the flashcards or give them clues by describing the pictures, e.g. *I can see one of these in picture B near the bed. In picture A it's on the desk.* NB there isn't an armchair or cupboard in the pictures.
Extension activity: learners describe one of the pictures to their partner who has to say which picture is being described, A or B. Alternatively, learners ask questions to discover which picture their partner has chosen.

KEY 1 desk 2 lamp 3 shelves 4 cupboard
5 armchair 6 mirror 7 laptop 8 carpet

3 Learners work in pairs. Check spelling is accurate.

KEY 1 desk 2 shelves 3 carpet 4 lamp 5 laptop

4 This is preparation for R&W6 where candidates read definitions and complete the word. If you think learners will find this difficult, you can pre-teach these words using flashcards.

KEY 1 bathroom 2 dining room 3 kitchen 4 living room

Reading (page 55)

5 This is preparation for R&W7 where candidates read a text and write the missing words. Here the missing words are supplied in the box which is not the case in the actual test. First get learners to read the whole text. They should decide which bedroom on page 54 is Zoe's.

NB the armchair and cupboard aren't visible in picture A.

KEY Picture A

6 Learners work individually and then compare with a partner.

KEY 1 got 2 do 3 of 4 but 5 because 6 have
7 me 8 from 9 some 10 all

7 You could describe your bedroom or your son's/daughter's bedroom to model the activity. Encourage learners to use *I've got a... but I haven't got a... There's a... but there isn't a...*

KEY Open answers

8 Check learners understand the phrases in the box. NB Point out that *all the time* comes at the end of the sentence not before the verb. *My parents tell me to turn the TV off all the time.*

KEY Open answers

Writing (page 55)

9 This is a model answer for R&W9. Learners write the missing adjectives in pairs.

KEY 1 long 2 bigger 3 happy 4 sad 5 old

10 Learners write their email in class/ for homework. They are often asked to imagine a scenario in Part 9 – remind them that the emails don't have to be factually accurate. They can invent as much as they like!

KEY Sample answer

> Dear Tommy,
> Our new house is in the city. I have a quite small bedroom, but I like it. I didn't want to move but now I like city life. There is so much to do.
> Write soon, Anna

At home

Grammar (page 56)

11 Look at the pictures. Establish that A is a farmer and B is a film director. Ask where they think the houses are. Ask which house/car/man is old? (Picture A). Learners decide who said each of the statements. Don't go into grammar explanations yet.
Then draw a timeline on the board illustrating the first statement.
1875 ——————→ NOW FUTURE
Explain that the Present Perfect is used for things which are unfinished. Ask concept questions. *Is the farmer still living in the same house?*
It's also used when the time is unknown or unimportant as in sentences 7 and 8. Draw a timeline to illustrate this.
??????? ——————→ NOW FUTURE
Ask, *Do we know which cities the film director lived in or when?* Highlight the form: present of 'have' + past participle. Point out that for many verbs the past participle is the same form as the Past Simple, e.g. *studied, made, had*. They can check the list of irregular verbs on p. 111.

KEY 1A 2B 3B 4A 5A 6A 7B 8B

12 Elicit the answers and give examples for each one, e.g. *It's been sunny for two weeks. I haven't been to the cinema for two weeks. Elena's been ill since yesterday.* Point out the contracted form. Here *it's* means *it has. Elena's = Elena has.* We can use *for* with both the Past Simple and the Present Perfect but we can only use *since* with the Present Perfect.

KEY **Since**: 2005, last month, Christmas, November, yesterday
For: two weeks, 5 years, one hour, a long time

13 Learners write true sentences using for or since. They can refer to the Grammar Bank for help.

KEY Open answers

Complete the Rules!
Complete the rules with the class and translate any unfamiliar terminology.

KEY **1** Present Perfect **2** Past Simple **3** Present Perfect

14 Do the first one as an example. Then get learners to work in pairs.

KEY **1** moved **2** haven't seen **3** gave **4** 's been **5** 've known **6** first met

15 Unscramble the questions with the class. Drill focusing on natural rhythm and intonation.

KEY **1** How long have you lived in your house?
2 How many years have you lived in this town?
3 How many times have you visited another country? **4** Have you ever been to London?

16 Learners ask and answer in pairs.

KEY Open answers

Listening (page 57)

(15) See recording script on page 49.

17 Look at the picture of the castle. Ask which country learners think this is in. Tell learners about a castle/old building you have visited before getting learners to talk in pairs. Find out if the class have all visited any local monuments/old buildings. Ask if learners enjoy visiting old buildings

KEY Open answers

18 This is the same task as L5. L5 is always a monologue. Look at the notes with the class before playing the recording to identify the kind of information missing.

KEY **1** a place **2** a place **3** a place **4** a time **5** a price

19-20 Point out the distracting information, i.e. 'bedrooms', '5.30', '£4.50'. In the test there isn't a distractor for every item.

KEY **1** garden **2** shop **3** kitchen **4** 5.45 **5** 3.25

Speaking (page 57)

21-22 Give learners time to think about their perfect house. Show pictures and say which house you like best and why. Choose a few learners to present their plans to the class or ask for volunteers. This is preparation for S1 where learners are expected to produce a short 'long turn' of four to five sentences. They aren't expected to speak for one minute.

KEY Open answers

▶▶▶ Internet Project ◀◀◀

Learners read about a day in the life of a boy living in a Chinese village and answer the questions that follow. Highlight the fact that where he's living now there isn't a proper bathroom (no running water) and he has to share a bedroom with his parents but that they are moving to a new house soon.

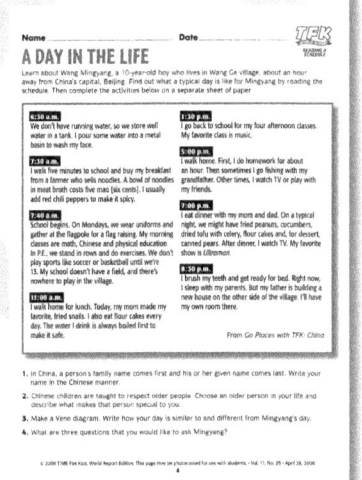

25

UNIT 12

KET topic	Shopping
Vocabulary	Prices; Shopping
Grammar	Passive forms
Reading	**R&W1** Matching notices; Pocket money: **R&W5** Multiple-choice cloze
Writing	Buying presents: **R&W9** email; Expressing thanks
Listening	Buying presents: **L4** Gap-fill
Speaking	Asking for simple information

Warmer (page 58)

1 Look at the picture. This could be a department store or a shop which sells TVs and other electrical goods. Learners discuss the questions in pairs and then as a whole class.

KEY Open answers

Vocabulary (page 58)

2 Find the items in the picture or use flashcards to elicit the words. Then learners decide how much they think each item costs. Practise saying the prices. NB Make sure they say *two hundred AND ninety six euros*.

KEY Open answers

3 (16) See recording script on page 49. Learners listen and check the prices.

KEY 1E 2C 3A 4B 5D

4 Learners match the words and definitions. You could get learners to check their answers using a learner dictionary.

KEY 1 pay 2 discount 3 cost 4 cash 5 save

5 Learners complete the sentences. They can check their answers by listening to the recording from ex. 2 again. Ask the class to say *stop* when they hear the answers.

KEY 1 cost 2 save 3 pay 4 cash 5 discount

6 Show pictures of the cars and houses, electrical items and say how much they cost. Elicit *expensive*. Then elicit sentences about the items on page 58 using *too*, *very* and *quite*. Make sure learners understand the difference between *too* and *very*. Learners work in pairs discussing the prices of the items in the catalogues.

KEY Open answers

Reading (page 59)

7 Check learners understand *pet shop*. Then get them to read the notices quickly for gist.

KEY H

8 This reading is based on R&W1. Look at the example with the class and then get them to work individually. They can check their answers in pairs.

KEY 1C 2A 3F 4G 5E

Listening (page 59)

(17) See recording script on page 49.

9 This activity is preparation for L4. It's important to train learners to try and predict the type of information missing before they listen.

KEY A2 B4 C1 D0 E5 F3 G extra

10 Play the recording twice. Learners compare in pairs and then check their answers using the recording script.

KEY 1 £13.50 2 Mayhem 3 shoes 4 cinema 5 Wednesday

11 Demonstrate the activity by describing one of your favourite presents. This gives practice in extended speaking. In the speaking test learners aren't expected to speak for one minute, although there is an opportunity for a short *long turn* in S1.

Speaking (page 60)

12 This information gap activity is preparation for S2. In the actual test candidates have to form questions from prompts. Here they just need to put the words in the correct order. Divide the class into As and Bs. Ask As to form the questions for Student A and B's to form Student B's questions.

KEY **Student A: 1** How much do the puppies cost? **2** What colour are the puppies? **3** Do they sell other animals? **4** Is the shop open on Sunday?

26

How much is it?

Student B: 1 What are the prices like? **2** Do they sell clothes for skaters? **3** Is it a big shop? **4** What time does the shop open on Sunday?

13 Ask student As to study the information about the skateboard shop and Student Bs to look at the pet shop. Tell them not to read the other information. Pair As and Bs together. They take turns to ask and answer.

KEY Open answers

Reading (page 60)

14-15 This is a prediction task to train learners to gist read texts for R&W5. Check learners understand *pocket money*, and then ask the class if they agree with the statements. Learners read the text quickly to confirm if they were right about sentences 1-3.

KEY **1**F **2**F **3**F – both boys and girls

16 Look at the example together. Remind learners to read the whole sentence before choosing the options and to check the text makes sense. Learners can compare answers in small groups. Two of these items (2 and 5) focus on the use of countables and uncountables. If learners get these wrong, refer them to Grammar Bank Unit 6. Highlight the importance of learning which preposition follows a verb, e.g. *spend on*.

KEY **1**B **2**C **3**A **4**C **5**B **6**A

17 Learners discuss the questions in pairs.

KEY Open answers

Grammar (page 61)

18 Write an example of the Present Simple passive on the board, e.g. *Ferraris are made in Italy.* Contrast this with *They make Ferraris in Italy.* The passive is more natural here because the focus is on the cars not the people who make them. Highlight the form *be + past participle*. Now get learners to tick the passive sentences.

KEY Sentences 1 and 4 are passive.

Complete the rules!

KEY **1** be **2** past participle

19 Check learners understand the verbs can be active or passive, present or past.

KEY **1** was made **2** made, are **3** was built, built **4** wasn't written, wrote **5** was given, gave

20 Write *made in, made of, made by* on the board and check learners know the difference before they write their sentences.

KEY Open answers

Writing (page 61)

21 This is preparation for R&W9. This trains learners to think about the information they must include.

KEY A, D, E

22 Learners write their emails in class or for homework.

KEY Sample answer

> Dear Charlie,
> Let's buy Andrew a hat because he always wears one. I can go shopping with you on Saturday morning. I think we need £15 to buy a hat.
> See you on Saturday.
> Liam

23-24 This is based on R&W7. Get learners to identify the type of word missing. Is it a pronoun, adverb, preposition? Talk about thank you letters with the class. Do they write emails or send letters?

KEY **1** it **2** some **3** lots **4** on **5** to **6** watched

▶▶▶ Internet Project ◀◀◀

This has a shopping list showing the cost of everyday items in Britain. Learners can use this information to compare prices with the same things in their own country. (you can use a website which converts currencies).

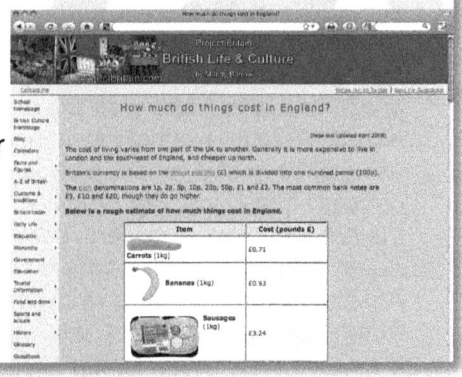

EXAM BANK pp 62-63

R&W3
1B 2G 3C 4E 5H

R&W7
1 of **2** where **3** was **4** have **5** my **6** to **7** lots **8** but **9** is **10** me

L3
(18) See recording script on page 50.
1A 2C 3B 4B 5A

S2
Open answers

UNIT 13

KET topics	The natural world; Weather
Vocabulary	Animals; Weather
Grammar	Present Perfect with *just, yet* and *already*
Reading	An elephant park: **R&W4** Right/Wrong/Doesn't say
Writing	Talking about the weather: **R&W9** Email
Listening	The natural world: **L1** Multiple-choice pictures
Speaking	Asking about animals: **S2** interactive task

Warmer (page 64)

1   Check learners know *snake* and *pet* before they discuss the questions in pairs. Possible aids: flashcards of animals: puppy, kitten, chicken, horse, goat. Feedback: Find out how many learners have a dog, cat, etc. Does anyone have an unusual pet?

KEY Open answers

Grammar (page 64)

2   Pre-teach *farm* and use the flashcards to elicit the animal words. NB not all the animal words presented in this unit are on the KET wordlist (e.g. *snake, kitten, puppy*) but they are all accessible at A2 and relevant to this age group. Look at the list of Adam's jobs with the class. Ask questions *Has Adam already taken the goats for a walk?* and elicit the response *No, he hasn't*. Write an example sentence about Adam using *already* and *yet* on the board. Ask concept questions, e.g. *When did Adam clean the parrot's cage?* Answer: *Today*. *When does Adam need to take the goats for a walk?* Answer: *Today*. Learners write sentences about Adam using 'already' and 'yet'.

KEY **1** Adam has already cleaned the parrot's cage. He has already given food to the chickens and he has already washed the puppy. **2** Adam hasn't taken the goats for a walk yet and he hasn't found the lost kitten yet. He hasn't brushed the horses yet.

3   This exercise introduces *just*. Look at the first example with the class. Explain that 'just' is the best word here because it's used to describe an action which finished very recently. Using the Grammar Bank to help them, learners complete the sentences in pairs.

KEY **1** just **2** already **3** just **4** already **5** yet **6** yet

4   Write some daily activities on the board, e.g. *have breakfast, watch TV, have a shower*. Tell learners the things you've already done/haven't done yet. Learners can ask and answer questions in pairs. *Have you had breakfast yet?* etc.

KEY Open answers

Vocabulary (page 65)

5   Learners can do this in pairs. Encourage them to guess if they're not sure. Feedback: practise the pronunciation.

KEY **1** J **2** A **3** F **4** I **5** E **6** H **7** G **8** D **9** C **10** B

6   Elicit the answers. Teach the new words by describing where there are deserts/ jungles/ forest and what they're like, e.g. *In Saudi Arabia there's a lot of desert. Deserts are very hot with lots of sand and not many trees. The Sahara is the most famous desert.* You could highlight the difference between *dessert* and *desert* as this is something learners often get confused.

KEY **1** camels, lizards **2** bears **3** parrots, monkeys **4** tigers **5** dolphins, whales **6** cows, sheep

7   Learners work in pairs to write the missing words. Check the spelling of *foggy*.

KEY **1** sun **2** rainy **3** cloud **4** foggy **5** snowy **6** wind **7** icy **8** storm

8   Learners work in pairs asking and answering the questions.

KEY Open answers

Reading (page 66)

9   Discuss with the class what they think an *elephant park* is and where this might be.

KEY Asia & Africa

10   This is the same task as R&W4 although in the actual test there are 7 questions plus an example. Learners work individually and then compare answers in pairs. Tell them not to worry about any unfamiliar words yet. Remind them to underline the parts of the text which give the answers.

KEY **1** A **2** C **3** B **4** A **5** A

Mother Nature

11 Learners can use their dictionaries to check the meaning of unknown words. Ask learners if they would like to visit the elephant park or send money to help the elephants.
KEY Open answers

Writing (page 66)

12 This task prepares learners for R&W9. It encourages them to think carefully about the kind of information required.
KEY Sentences 3, 5, 6

13 Learners can write their emails in class or for homework. Make sure they proofread their work and check it's the right length.
KEY Sample answer

> Dear Kim,
> I like summer best because we have a long holiday then. In winter it gets dark very early. When it's raining I usually go to my friend's house.
> From
> Kelly

Listening (page 67)

(19) See recording script on page 50.

14-16 This is based on L1. In the actual test there are 5 multiple-choice questions. Look at the pictures and ask learners to describe them. Tell learners to read the questions carefully before they listen.
KEY 1B 2B 3A

Speaking (page 67)

17 This is preparation for S2. Pre-teach 'only' child. Get learners to make questions in pairs. Extension task: Learners use the same questions to ask/answer about each others' pets.

▶▶▶ Internet Project ◀◀◀

Learners click on a fact file for a country or region e.g. Alaska. They should then find one fact about the weather and the animals that live there to report back to the class

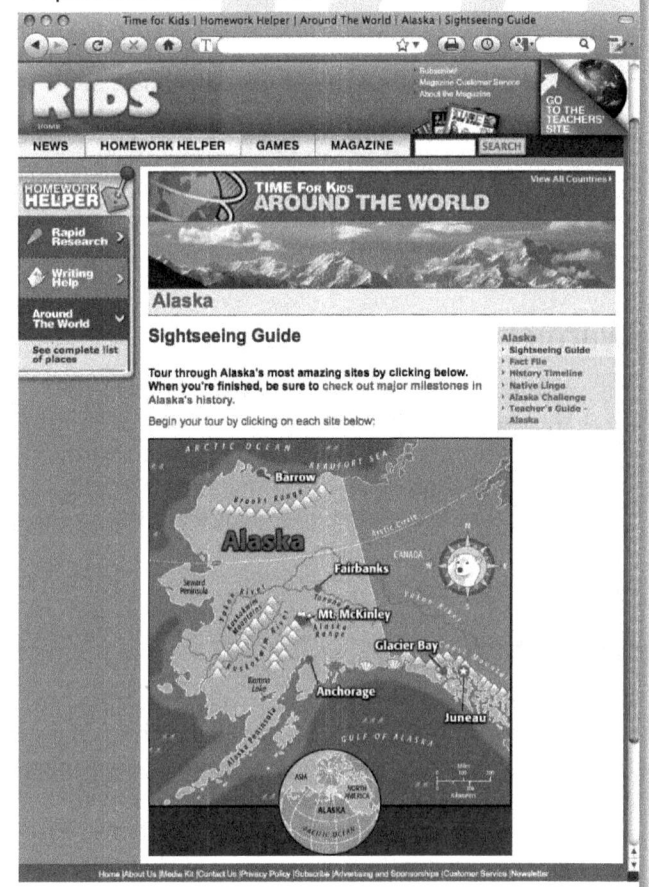

A spot the difference activity showing a winter scene.

UNIT 14

KET topics	People; Personal feelings, opinions and experiences
Vocabulary	Adjectives for describing qualities
Grammar	*Will* future situations; Relative pronouns
Reading	My best friend: **R&W7** Open cloze
Writing	Describing people's qualities
Listening	Expressing likes and dislikes: **L2** Matching
Speaking	People's qualities; Expressing degrees of certainty

Warmer (page 68)

1 Learners discuss the comments in pairs and then as a whole class. This task introduces *will* for future predictions. Demonstrate the activity by going through the first question with the class. Let them continue answering the questions individually.

KEY Open answers

Grammar (page 68)

2 Learners ask and answer in pairs. Get them to use the full question and answer forms. Drill sentences A-D focusing on correct sentence stress. You can extend the discussion with a strong group by asking further questions, e.g. *Where do you think you will live? How do you know you won't meet your future husband/wife at school?*
Feedback: Compare the class's answers by getting those who put A, etc. to put their hands up.

KEY Open answers

3 Learners write sentences and use the Grammar Bank to help.

KEY Open answers

Complete the Rules!

KEY **1** future **2** infinitive **3** to

Reading (page 69)

4 This task is preparation for R&W7. It trains learners to read the text before attempting to fill the gaps.

KEY **1** Harriet is funny, popular and lively. **2** Hannah is quieter and not as popular as Harriet.

5 Learners work individually. Remind them to think about what kind of word is missing – a verb/preposition, etc. Tell them to read the whole sentence to check it makes sense. Learners compare answers in pairs.

KEY **1** is **2** for **3** any **4** a/per **5** On **6** because **7** at **8** more **9** as **10** be/make

6 Learners work in pairs to find the opposites. You may need to pre-teach *lively* and *serious*. Encourage them to guess if they're not sure or get learners to check in their dictionaries. Feedback: go through the answers and practise the pronunciation. Show learners where the main stress is in each adjective.

KEY **1** quiet **2** popular **3** boring **4** funny **5** different

Vocabulary (page 69)

7 This task is preparation for R&W6 where learners have to read definitions and complete the missing words. Learners complete the sentences and then check their answers in pairs or with a dictionary.

KEY **1** friendly **2** naughty **3** kind **4** happy **5** brave **6** clever

8 Elicit the answers. Remind learners to make a note of the adjectives and their opposites and to learn them at home. NB not all of these adjectives are on the KET wordlist but are high frequency and conceptually easy.
Extension task: learners write sentences comparing themselves with their best friend or brother/sister, e.g. *I'm quite quiet but my sister is very lively.*

KEY unkind, unfriendly, unhappy

9 Pre-teach *clown* before learners complete the sentences in pairs.

KEY *Possible answers:* **1** clever **2** friendly **3** brave **4** brave **5** happy **6** unfriendly

Writing (page 70)

10-11 If you have a large class this would be better done in groups of six to eight. This is an opportunity for an extended piece of writing – which learners are not expected to do at KET. If

30

She's very funny

you have a weak class you could omit this task. It could also be done for homework.

KEY Sample answer

> My best friend is called Alex. I've known her for three years and we are in the same class at school. We also live near each other and we go to school together every morning.
> On Saturdays I go ice skating and she goes swimming, but we see each other after.
> Alex is my best friend because she is so nice and friendly. We have lots of fun together and can talk about anything.

KEY Open answers

Grammar (page 70)

12 Get learners to complete the task and check their answers using the Grammar Bank. This will also help them to complete the rules.

KEY **1** who **2** that **3** where **4** where **5** that **6** which

Complete the Rules!
1 which, that   **2** who, that   **3** where

13 Write *A... is someone/a person who...; A... is a thing which/that...* and *A... is a place where...* on the board for learners to refer to when writing their sentences.
Extension activity: ask learners to think of an everyday object, person or place, or bring pictures in for them to choose from. Learners take turns to describe their object, without naming it. The others have to guess what it is, e.g. *This is a place where people play football. People also take their dogs for a walk here.* Answer: a park.

KEY *Possible answers:* **1** A hotel is a place where people stay on holiday. **2** A journalist is a person who writes articles for newspapers and magazines. **3** A camera is a machine which we use to take photographs. **4** A factory is a place where things are produced. **5** A farmer is a person who grows food and keeps animals to sell. **6** An ambulance is a vehicle which takes people to hospital.

Speaking (page 71)

14-15 You may need to pre-teach *laugh, depend on, secret, truth, angry*. Learners rank the qualities individually. Learners should decide on the most important qualities for a friend. They can use the letters (A-J) when discussing this otherwise the grammar may get too complicated.
Feedback: find out which are considered the most important qualities by the class.

KEY Open answers

16 Demonstrate the task by eliciting a few possibilities for question 1, e.g. *go shopping, play football*, etc. Learners then complete the questions individually.

KEY Open answers

17-18 Demonstrate in open class. Get learners to ask you their questions. Drill the responses and then get learners to ask and answer in pairs. Tell learners some of your plans for the summer. Remind learners they should use the Present Continuous for plans, *may* for possibilities and *will* for predictions, e.g. *I'm going to Ireland this summer.* (plan); *I may go horse riding.* (possibility); *I'm sure I'll have a nice time.* (prediction).

KEY Open answers

Listening (page 71)

(20) See recording script on page 50.

19-21 This is based on L2. Play the recording twice and then let learners look at the recording script to check their answers.

KEY **1**B **2**G **3**E **4**F **5**A

▶▶▶ Internet Project ◀◀◀

This is an authentic interview with a young English teacher living in Japan, talking about her plans for next year. There's a worksheet to go with it. Learners will find this challenging

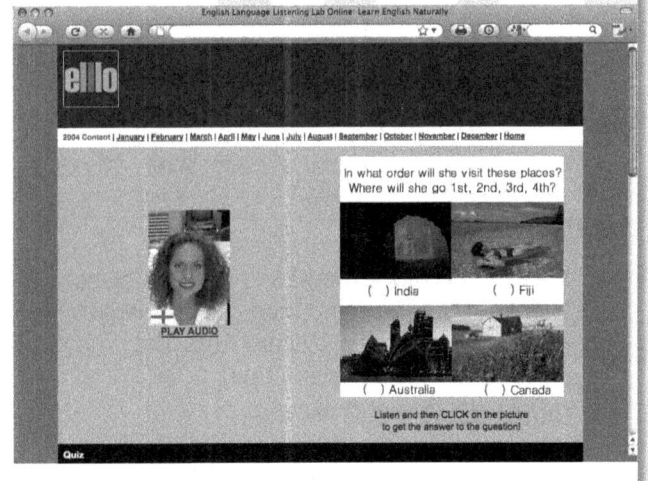

There's also a questionnaire you can print off with answers: 'Are you a good friend?'

UNIT 15

KET topic	Places and buildings
Vocabulary	Places in a town; Directions
Grammar	*Going to*: future plans; Imperatives: giving simple instructions
Reading	Giving information about places: **R&W7** Open cloze
Writing	Giving information about places: **R&W9** Note
Listening	About town: **L1** Multiple-choice pictures
Speaking	Making comparisons: village vs city

Warmer (page 72)

1 Learners discuss the questions with a partner. If learners already live in a big modern city, discuss what it would be like to live in a small town or village.

KEY Shanghai

Reading (page 72)

2 This is preparation for R&W7. Remind learners they need to read the whole text for gist before trying to fill any of the gaps. Point out that sometimes more than one answer is possible.

KEY food, things to see

3 Learners should work individually and then check their answers in pairs. Get them to read each sentence carefully and to look at the words before and after each gap to check it makes sense

KEY 1 lots 2 in/around 3 of 4 at 5 out
6 everywhere 7 There 8 best 9 all 10 never

Grammar (page 73)

4 Look at the model sentence with the class. Highlight the form and then get learners to decide if sentences A–D are true. They may need to refer back to the text.

KEY Sentences A and C are true.

5 The Present Continuous and *going to* are often interchangeable to talk about future plans, as are *will* and *going to* for predictions. It's not worth explaining small differences in meaning at this level.

KEY 2, 4, 5, 6, 7

Complete the Rules!

Learners do the exercise in pairs. They can use the Grammar Bank to help them complete the rules. Feedback: Explain that arrangements are plans you put in your diary and you use the Present Continuous for this. For more distant, long-term plans or intentions, use *going to*. In other cases you can use either.

KEY 1B 2A 3C 4B

Vocabulary (page 73)

6 Learners label the pictures. Check spelling and pronunciation.

KEY 1 museum 2 airport 3 library 4 market
5 theatre 6 castle 7 football stadium
8 cinema

7 This is preparation for S1 as learners may be asked to talk about their town or a place in their town.

KEY Open answers

Writing (page 73)

8 Tell learners to underline Rodrigo's questions. Then they write their emails in class or for homework.

KEY Sample answer

> I live in the country in northern France. There are lots of cottages here. There isn't much to do but there is a cinema. I like it because the air is clean and it's beautiful.

Grammar (page 74)

9 Give learners time to familiarise themselves with the map. Explain that *florist* is another word for *flower shop*. Learners complete the directions with the missing verbs.
Feedback: go through the answers and then explain that these verbs are imperatives. Remind the class they've heard lots of imperatives before, e.g. *Sit down, Work in pairs, Open your book*.

KEY 1 take 2 Get off 3 Cross 4 turn 5 Walk
6 don't go

I love my city

10 Learners practise giving directions. One learner could read the directions while their partner gives the directions and corrects them if they make a mistake.

KEY Open answers

11 Elicit some examples. Then ask learners to compare with a partner.

KEY Open answers

Speaking (page 74)

12-14 Check learners understand *village*. They should brainstorm ideas in pairs/small groups. Feedback: make a list on the board using learners' ideas. Find out how many learners want to live in a city/village. Demonstrate the activity by giving an example. Then learners work in pairs.

KEY Open answers

15-16 Check learners know what these places are. Explain *improve*. Learners can discuss this in small groups. Feedback: You could get one person in each group to report back to the class. Learners could vote on their preferred choice. Extension task: learners produce a bar chart showing how many people in the class think they need a skate park, etc.

KEY Open answers

Listening (page 75)

(21) See recording script on page 50.

17 This is preparation for L1. Get learners to study the pictures and read the questions carefully before listening. Brainstorm the words they think they will hear and write them on the board.

KEY *Possible answers:* **1** bag, bus, get off, get on, shopping **2** city, town, village **3** top floor, flat, garden, roof, ground floor, balcony **4** north, south, east west **5** opposite, next to, at the end of

18-19 Play the recording twice. Learners compare answers with a partner.
Ask learners which of the words on the board they heard.
Look at the recording script. Learners check their answers and check which words they heard.

KEY **1**C **2**B **3**A **4**A **5**A

▶▶▶ Internet Project ◀◀◀

Learners research a city in China or Japan. They click on the map and find three facts about the city.

EXAM BANK pp 76-77

R&W5
1C **2**B **3**B **4**A **5**C **6**B **7**A **8**A **9**B **10**C

R&W9
Sample answer

Dear Jude,
I'm going to the USA for my next holiday. I am going to visit New York so I will do lots of sightseeing. We're going to stay for ten days. I can't wait either.
Love
Alison

L5
(22) See recording script on page 51.
1 8.45 **2** Keeler **3** lion **4** 2.50 **5** mobile phone

S2
Open answers

Key to the GRAMMAR BANK

Unit 1 (page 78)
1 1 don't like   2 studies   3 works
   4 doesn't have   5 watches   6 plays
2 1 ~~His~~ Her   2 ~~Ours~~ Our   3 ~~His~~ Their   4 ~~It's~~ Its

Unit 2 (page 79)
1 1 Does your mother work?   2 Does your brother have blue eyes?   3 Is your sister married?   4 Do you watch TV after school?   5 Do your parents speak English?

Unit 3 (page 80)
1 1 don't have to get up early...   2 mustn't wear jeans   3 must get to
2 1 They are never late for school.   2 How often do you play basketball?   3 We sometimes go to school by bus.   4 They always have pasta for lunch.   5 Do you often do your homework at the weekend?

Unit 4 (page 81)
1 1 A Is   B is
   2 A Are   B I'm not
   3 A Is it   B it is
2 1 When do you play football?
   2 Why are you tired?
   3 What does your father do in his free time?

Unit 5 (page 82)
1 1 taller than   2 easier than   3 as hot as   4 less expensive
2 1 the wettest   2 the shortest   3 the most famous   4 the worst

Unit 6 (page 83)
1 1 some   2 any   3 a   4 an
2 1 much   2 many   3 much

Unit 7 (page 84)
1 1 had   2 didn't stay   3 watched   4 was   5 didn't go
2 1 ~~went~~ go   2 ~~you were~~ were you   3 ~~liked~~ like   4 ~~hadn't~~ didn't have   5 ~~What you did~~ What did you do

Unit 8 (page 85)
1 1 correct   2 ~~watching~~ watch   3 correct   4 correct

2 1 He was working when you phoned him
   2 Were they playing tennis yesterday afternoon?
   3 Was he living in Rome in 2009?   4 They weren't doing their homework when I arrived.
   5 I saw Sally when I was shopping.   6 She was taking the dog for a walk at six o'clock.

Unit 9 (page 86)
1 3 nice orange Indian cotton   4 cheap small silver Japanese
2 1 need to go   2 needs (or will need)   3 correct   4 Do you need   5 doesn't need   6 correct

Unit 10 (page 87)
1 Open answers
2 1 Shall   2 'm going   3 shall   4 may not   5 'm going

Unit 11 (page 88)
1 1 have known   2 have been   3 hasn't studied   4 Have you had   5 Have they ever been   6 haven't seen

Unit 12 (page 89)
1 1 was completed   2 was stolen   3 are cleaned   4 are given   5 wasn't born   6 were/are not invited
2 1 The last CD player was bought by my uncle.   2 The shoes were made in Thailand.   3 A new shop in the high street was opened.   4 My new dress was bought in the sale.   5 The shops in London are visited by thousands of tourists every year.

Unit 13 (page 90)
1 1 Have you already had dinner?   2 I haven't made my bed yet.   3 He's just won a million dollars.   4 She has already been to the supermarket.   5 We haven't invited Nina to the party yet.   6 I've just had an email from Daisy.

Unit 14 (page 91)
1 1 She'll marry   2 Will he win   3 I hope you'll   4 It won't be   5 Will you visit   6 They'll make
2 1 which   2 where   3 who   4 who   5 where   6 which

Unit 15 (page 92)
1 1 are going to open   2 is going to stay   3 is going to run   4 am going to buy   5 is going to meet
2 1 Don't go to sleep now.   2 Don't finish your homework.   3 Please tell me the answer.   4 Eat all the pizza.

Communication Bank

Key to the COMMUNICATION BANK

Communication Bank 1 (page 93)

(24) See recording script on page 51.
1 1 Bowling 2 12 3 North London 4 Acland House
2 1 What's 2 How do 3 How 4 do you go to 5 Where do you 6 Do you
3 Open answers
4 1 York 2 Eccleston 3 Swansea 4 Cambridge 5 Edinburgh
5 Open answers
6 1B 2A 3B 4B

Communication Bank 2 (page 93)

(25) See recording script on page 51.
1 1 22nd 2 2.30 3 Arkesden 4 library 5 £5.30
2 1 What date is that? 2 That's the 22nd, isn't it? 3 Sorry, I can't hear you very well. What time? 4 And which school is it at? 5 Sorry, Could you spell that again, please? 6 So we need to go by bus. 7 Do I need to bring anything? 8 How much? £5.15 or £5.50?
3 Open answers
4 Open answers

Communication Bank 3 (page 94)

(26) See recording script on page 51.
1 1 I'm not sure. Why? 2 Yes. I'd love to. What time shall I come? 3 I think she may be at her aunt's house. 4 That's a good idea. I'll bring a cake. 5 See you on Saturday.
2 Open answers
3 Open answers

Communication Bank 4 (page 95)

(27) See recording script on page 51.
1 1B 2C
2 1 at 2 by 3 to 4 at 5 Can 6 mustn't 7 can 8 can't 9 no 10 afraid 11 problem 12 fine 13 very 14 pity
3 Open answers
4 1 all are possible 2 C, D, E 3 all are possible 4 all are possible
(28) See recording script on page 52.
5 Open answers

Communication Bank 5 (page 96)

(29) See recording script on page 52.
1 Jon: That's a cool bag.
   Steve: Thanks very much. I really like it too.
   Jon: Where's it from?
   Steve: I think it's from a shop in London.
   Jon: Who gave it to you?
   Steve: My brother gave it to me for my birthday.
   Jon: Did he give you that scarf too?
   Steve: No, I bought that in a market last month.
2 Open answers
3 Open answers

Communication Bank 6 (page 96)

(30) See recording script on page 52.
1 1B 2A 3A 4C 5C 6A 7B 8A
2 Open answers
3 1 A, B, D 2 B, D 3 A, C, D

Communication Bank 7 (page 97)

(31) See recording script on page 52.
1 Doesn't like: 1, 4, 5
2 1 hate 2 don't mind 3 don't like 4 I'd prefer 5 favourite 6 special 7 worst 8 sad
3 Open answers

Communication Bank 8 (page 98)

(32) See recording script on page 52.
1 1C 2B 3A
2 1 couldn't 2 Weren't 3 was able to 4 couldn't
3 could read, was able to, could speak, could make
4 Open answers

Communication Bank 9 (page 99)

(33) See recording script on page 52.
1 1C 2C 3B
2 1 sure 2 may 3 may be 4 'll 5 hope 6 certain 7 won't 8 'll
3 Open answers

Communication Bank 10 (page 100)

(34) See recording script on page 52.
1 1A 2A 3B
2 Open answers
3 Open answers

Teacher's Book Communication Resource

	Basics
U1/CB1	greeting people and responding to greetings (in person and on the phone) *How are you? Fine, thank you.* Page 93
U1/CB1	introducing oneself and other people *This is... Pleased to meet you* Page 93
U2	asking for and giving personal details: (full) name, age, address, names of relatives and friends, etc. *My name's... I'm... years old.* Page 12
CB1	understanding and completing forms giving personal details *My address is...* Page 93
CB1	asking for and giving the spelling and meaning of words *How do you spell that?* Page 93
CB1/CB2	asking and telling people the time, day and/or date *It starts at...* Page 93
	Communication repair
CB2	asking for repetition and clarification *Could you say that again, please?* Page 94
CB2	re-stating what has been said *That's..., right?* Page 94
	Verb forms
U1	asking for and giving information about routines and habits *Scott gets up very early.* Page 8
U1	understanding and giving information about everyday activities *What time do Anna and Scott do these things?* Page 10
U4	talking about what people are doing at the moment *She's singing.* Page 23
U7/U13	talking about past events and states in the past, recent activities and completed actions *Last year Kate went to Salou.* Page 37 *Adam has already washed the puppy.* Page 64
U8	understanding and producing simple narratives *Last Sunday it was a beautiful day so Dan's parents had a barbecue.* Page 42
U11	reporting what people say *My parents often tell me to tidy my room.* Page 55
U14	talking about future situations *I don't think I'll see my friends at the weekend.* Page 68
U15/U10	talking about future plans or intentions *Georgia is visiting London next week.* Page 52 *I'm going to live here all my life.* Page 73
U14	making predictions *I don't think I'll see my friends at the weekend.* Page 68
U15	following and giving simple instructions *Turn left.* Page 74

U1, **U2**, etc.: these refer to the units of the Student's Book.
CB1, **CB2**, etc.: these refer to sections of the Communication Bank in the Student's Book.

Communication Bank

Modal verbs

U3	expressing obligation and lack of obligation *We have to wear a uniform.* Page 16
U3/CB6	asking and giving/refusing permission to do something *You mustn't eat in the classroom.* Page 17 *Do you mind if I borrow your pen?* Page 97
U9	expressing needs and wants *Do you need any help?* Page 47
U5/CB8	expressing (in)ability in the present and in the past *I can play basketball.* Page 29 *I couldn't do all my homework last night.* Page 98
U10	talking about (im)probability and (im)possibility *We may watch the tennis this evening.* Page 52
U8	giving advice *You should stay in bed.* Page 41
U8	giving warnings and stating prohibitions *You mustn't run.* Page 41

Talking about... (topic-related vocab)

U3	describing education *We study Maths four times a week.* Page 18
U2/U15	describing people (personal appearance, qualities) *His hair is quite long and straight.* Page 14 *She's very funny.* Page 69
U6	talking about food and ordering meals *I'll have salad to start with, please.* Page 33
U13	talking about the weather *Today it's sunny.* Page 65
U8	talking about one's health *I've got a headache.* Page 41
U6	asking for and giving travel information *Kate prefers travelling by plane.* Page 37
U6	asking for and giving simple information about places
U15	*My house is behind the cinema.* Page 38 *It's the capital of Argentina.* Page 72
U11	identifying and describing accommodation (houses, flats, rooms, furniture, etc.) *My bedroom is quite small* Page 55
U12	identifying and describing simple objects (shape, size, weight, colour, purpose or use, etc.) *It was made in India.* Page 59
CB5	asking and answering questions about personal possessions *My brother gave it to me.* Page 96
U4/CB7	expressing preferences, likes and dislikes (especially about hobbies and leisure activities) *I like watching TV.* Page 22 *I'd prefer to stay at home.* Page 97
U9	buying things (costs and amounts)
U12	*How much is the dress?* Page 46 *It costs £59.99* Page 58
U12	understanding simple signs and notices *Please don't touch the animals.* Page 59

37

	Functions
U5	making comparisons and expressing degrees of difference *Golf is more dangerous than skiing.* Page 27
U6	making and granting/refusing simple requests *Can you cut me a slice of cake, please?* Page 32
CB3	making and responding to offers and suggestions *Shall I ask Erin too?* Page 94
U10	expressing and responding to thanks *Thank you for the invitation.* Page 53
CB3	giving and responding to invitations *Would you like to come to my house?* Page 94
U15	asking/telling people to do something *Turn the music down!* Page 74
CB4	making and responding to apologies and excuses *I'm sorry I can't come to my piano lesson.* Page 95
CB5	paying compliments *That's a cool bag.* Page 96
CB4	sympathising *Oh dear!* Page 96
CB7	talking about feelings *It makes me feel...* Page 97
CB9	expressing opinions and making choices *I'm sure I will get a car when I'm 17.* Page 99
U15	expressing degrees of certainty and doubt *I probably will.* Page 68
U15/CB10	asking the way and giving directions *From the station take the number 7 bus.* Page 74 *Go straight on.* Page 100

Answer key to the Skills & Vocab Maximiser

See pages 53-57 for the Recording Scripts to the Skills and Vocab Maximiser. All Track numbers relate to the Audio CD-ROM.

Unit 1 (page 6)

1 Monday, Tuesday, Wednesday, Thursday, Friday, Saturday, Sunday
2 Open answers
3 1C January 2H February 3A March 4F April 5J May 6E June 7K July 8B August 9D September 10G October 11L November 12I December
4 Open answers
5 1C swimming 2A by bike 3D get up 4B plays
6 1 gets up 2 shower 3 breakfast 4 takes 5 lunch 6 plays 7 finishes 8 homework 9 watches 10 bed
7-9 Open answers

Exam Practice (page 8)

R&W3 1C 2C 3B 4A
R&W7 1 in 2 at 3 to 4 After 5 In 6 a 7 before 8 On 9 is
L1 (3) 1B 2C 3C
S1 (4) Open answers

Unit 2 (page 10)

1 1 babies 2 children 3 men 4 grandchildren 5 women 6 wives 7 people 8 families
2 1B 2E 3C 4D 5A
3 [word search grid]
4 Open answers
5 A 1 strong, fat, big, heavy 2 small, thin, short, light B 1 thin, tall 2 small, light
6 1 long, straight, black 2 short, curly 3 long, wavy 4 short, dark
7 1 Amy's best friend's name's Ella 2 Amy's friends are all tall 3 Amy's got dark 4 Amy's friends have got fair hair.
8 1 This, His, He's 2 This, Her, She's 3 This, Her, She's 4 This, His, He's
9-10 Open answers

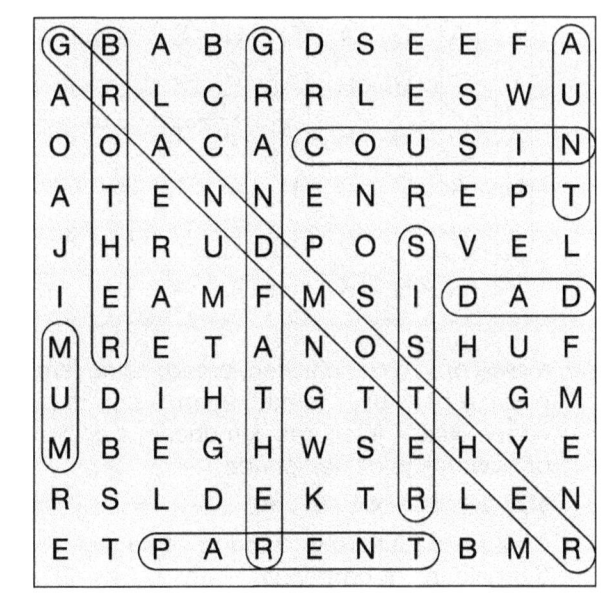

Exam Practice (page 12)

R&W5 1B 2C 3A 4A 5B 6A 7B 8B
R&W9 Sample answer

> I usually see my grandparents at weekends. My grandmother is 64 and my grandfather is 66. My grandmother has blonde hair and is very short. My grandfather has short grey hair and is quite tall.

L4 (5) 1 Morrissey 2 67 3 Australia 4 5 (3 brothers, 2 sisters) 5 green
S1 (6) 1 surname 2 do you spell 3 old are you 4 you born 5 brothers and sisters have you got? 6 your favourite

Unit 3 (page 14)

1 1B Geography 2D History 3E Science 4F Maths 5C Music 6A Art
2 1G room 2C field 3B room 4D room 5F field 6H room 7B office 8E room
3 1A 2C 3A 4B 5C 6B
4 Open answers
5 1 computer 2 blackboard 3 desk 4 bin 5 chair 6 bookshelves 7 ruler 8 pen 9 window 10 rucksack
6 1 bin 2 pens 3 board 4 computer 5 rucksacks, desk
7 1A 2B 3B 4A 5B
8 1 do 2 are 3 do 4 do 5 are 6 do 7 do 8 Is

Exam Practice (page 16)

R&W1 1F 2D 3H 4A 5C
R&W7 1 are 2 a 3 starts 4 have 5 of 6 at 7 anything 8 do
L2 (7) 1B 2A 3G 4H 5C
S2 (8) 1 No, 11 -14s 2 short story 3 500-1000 words 4 March 17 5 100 books for school library

Unit 4 (page 18)

1

Across: 2 COOK, 4 CHAT, 6 KEYBOARD, 7 MAGAZINE
Down: 1 PROGRAMME, 3 INSTRUMENT, 5 HOBBY

2

	Verb (noun)	Activity (noun)	Person
1	sing	singing	singer
2	paint	painting	painter
3	write	writing	writer
4	play	playing	player
5	dance	dancing	dancer
6	swim	swimming	swimmer
7	cook	cooking	cook (irregular)

3 *play*: the guitar, computer games, a sport, the drums, football;
do: photography, a sport, a painting, hobby;
practise: the guitar, the drums,

4 1 play 2 play 3 practise 4 play 5 does 6 practising

5 1 making a phone call 2 sending a message 3 reading a newspaper 4 watching a cartoon 5 taking a photograph 6 listening to a MP3 player

6-7 Open answers

Exam Practice (page 20)

R&W7 1 are 2 a 3 starts 4 have 5 of 6 at 7 anything 8 do

R&W8 1 6 2 bus 3 (outside) supermarket 4 5 5 dance shoes

L3 (9) 1B 2A 3A 4B 5A

S2 (10) 1 how to draw cartoons 2 1 November 3 City Art College 4 Yes 5 Call 897765

Unit 5 (page 22)

1 1 takes 2 lose 3 enter 4 win

2 1D 2C 3B 4E 5F 6A

3 1 swimmer 2 skier 3 hockey player 4 golfer 5 climber 6 basketball player

4 ...*er*: quicker, faster, smaller, slower, bigger; ...*ier*: easier, angrier, funnier; *more*...: difficult, boring, popular, dangerous, exciting; *irregular*: good (better), bad (worse), fun (more fun)

5 1A 2J 3D 4F 5E 6B 7I 8G 9H 10C

6 1B 2A 3E 4C 5D

7 1 do 2 Is 3 are 4 is 5 do 6 is

Exam Practice (page 24)

R&W4 1C 2B 3A 4C 5B 6A 7B

R&W9 Sample answer

> Yes, I'd love to play basketball with you. I'm free after school at 4 p.m. Let's meet in the café outside the sports centre. See you later.

L5 (11) 1 playground 2 8.45 3 Oakham 4 supermarket 5 0998765234

S2 (12) 1 West Park 2 Yes (large, 25 metres) 3 Yes, in the summer 4 beginners 5 River Street

Unit 6 (page 26)

1 Word search with: STRAWBERRY, ONION, POTATO, LEMON, etc.

2 *a slice of...*: roast chicken, bread, cake, lemon, pizza; *a bowl of...*: tomato soup; *a cup of...*: coffee, water, juice, tea, lemonade; *a bottle of...*: water, juice, lemonade

3 1D 2B 3C 4A 5F 6E

4 1 waitress 2 thirsty 3 fridge 4 sugar 5 breakfast 6 barbecue

5 1G 2D 3E 4I 5B 6A 7F 8C 9J 10H

Answer key to the Skills & Vocab Maximiser

6 1C 2W 3C 4W 5C 6C 7W 8C

7 **1** What do you usually have for breakfast? **2** How much chocolate do you eat? **3** What's your favourite type of fruit? **4** How often do you go to restaurants? **5** Do you eat a lot of fast food? **6** Do you sometimes cook dinner for your family?

Exam Practice (page 28)

R&W3 1E 2G 3H 4D 5B

R&W8 **1** 20 Bridge Street **2** 6 **3** Sunday **4** 2 **5** 01226 456456

L1 (13) 1B 2C 3B

S1 (14) **1** cooking **2** can you **3** learn to **4** in your family **5** home cooking... restaurant

Unit 7 (page 30)

1 **1** ship **2** train **3** car **4** taxi **5** bicycle/bike **6** lorry **7** motorcycle/motorbike **8** coach/bus **9** underground **10** tram

2 **1** by **2** off/on **3** in **4** on

3 **1** break **2** brought **3** bought **4** cut **5** did **6** fell **7** found **8** gave **9** grew **10** had **11** lost **12** made **13** met **14** put **15** ran **16** said **17** sold **18** spoke **19** spent **20** swum **21** took **22** taught **23** told **24** thought **25** won **26** wrote

4 **1** bought **2** took **3** put **4** made **5** won **6** have **7** taught **8** met

5 1H 2D 3E 4C 5B 6G 7A 8F

6 **1** in front **2** next **3** on the corner **4** behind **5** opposite **6** near

7 Open answers

Exam Practice (page 32)

R&W2 1A 2B 3C 4B 5A

R&W7 **1** of **2** too **3** than **4** was **5** would **6** a

L2 (15) 1B 2C 3F 4H 5A

S2 (16) **1** Tall Trees **2** No, it's open all year **3** Yes, there's a café and a shop **4** Yes, there's space for 200 tents **5** 2 kilometres

Unit 8 (page 34)

1

```
A M B U L A N C E
N S E R F R T A B
E A T D P S H C Z
H O S P I T A L N
W U L T O C X I U
D T N O G E I V R
M E K D S C J N S
D O C T O R Y I E
```

2

have	an accident, a temperature, a rest, an appointment, a headache, a problem
feel	healthy, tired, sick, worried, ill, better
make	an appointment
take	a temperature, medicine

3 **1** broken **2** black **3** stomach **4** temperature **5** cut **6** cough

4 **1** lie **2** clean **3** comb **4** wash **5** have **6** get

5 **1** ear **2** eye **3** nose **4** tooth **5** mouth **6** neck **7** finger **8** hand **9** arm **10** stomach **11** leg **12** toe **13** foot

6 **1** fingers, toes **2** neck **3** mouth **4** ears **5** feet **6** stomach

7 1A 2C 3B 4C

8 1D 2E 3A 4C 5B

Exam Practice (page 36)

R&W5 1B 2C 3A 4C 5B 6C 7B 8C

R&W9 Sample answer

My house is about a mile from school so it's not very far. Please come around four o'clock. Can you bring me a list of all the homework? Thanks.

L3 (17) 1A 2C 3C 4A 5B

S1 (18) **1** colds **2** stay healthy **3** sleep **4** miss school **5** sport **6** dangerous activities

Unit 9 (page 38)

1 **1** hat **2** sunglasses **3** T-shirt **4** gloves **5** watch **6** belt **7** shorts **8** socks **9** boots **10** pocket

2 **1** orange **2** white, black **3** blue **4** red **5** yellow **6** pink **7** brown **8** purple **9** green **10** grey

3-4 Open answers

5 These trousers are too tight, These trousers are too long, This skirt is too big- **1** shorts **2** T-shirt **3** scarf **4** shirt/blouse **5** coat **6** tights **7** jumper **8** (leather) jacket **9** trousers **10** skirt

6 1C 2D 3B 4A

7 Open answers

Exam Practice (page 40)

R&W1 1B 2D 3E 4G 5C

R&W6 **1** expensive **2** silver **3** wallet **4** cotton **5** uniform

L5 (19) **1** Wycliffe **2** Dark green **3** 12.99 **4** small **5** Saturday

S2 (20) **1** Red **2** 101 Oxford Street (one hundred and one *or* one-oh-one) **3** fashionable clothes for young people **4** 5th January **5** 9.30 a.m. - 8.30 p.m.

Unit 10 (page 42)

1

Crossword:
- 1 down: MAGAZINE
- 2 across: PLAY
- 3 across: WEBSITE
- 4 down: EXHIBITION
- 5 across: ARTICLE
- 6 across: PROGRAMMES
- down: SCREEN

2 1D 2A 3C 4B

3 1B chat 2D text 3A download 4C click

4 1C 2B 3C 4A 5B 6C

5 1 circus 2 singer 3 dancer 4 classical music 5 rock concert 6 clown 7 club 8 museum 9 cartoon 10 actor

6 1A 2B 3B 4A

7 Open answers

Exam Practice (page 44)

R&W3 1H 2A 3F 4E 5G

R&W8 1 (Saturday) 14 July 2 White Stadium 3 bus 4 £10 5 Kylie's dad

L1 (21) 1B 2C 3B

S1 (22) 1 types of TV programmes 2 actor 3 How often 4 film... why

Unit 11 (page 46)

1 1 stairs 2 garage 3 lift 4 gate 5 DVD player 6 washing machine 7 roof 8 radio

2 1 DVD player 2 washing machine 3 radio 4 garage, gate 5 roof

3 1D 2E 3B 4C 5F 6A

4 1 broken 2 caught 3 driven 4 eaten 5 fallen 6 found 7 grown 8 had 9 known 10 made 11 met 12 ridden 13 sent 14 taken 15 thought 16 written

5 1 sent 2 made 3 eaten 4 ridden 5 had/taken

6-9 Open answers

Exam Practice (page 48)

R&W4 1A 2A 3C 4B 5B 6A 7C

R&W9 Sample answer

> My bedroom is purple and white. I have a few film posters on the walls, but I don't have any pop stars. I really like my room because it is somewhere that I can relax.

L2 (23) 1H 2B 3C 4A 5D

S2 (24) 1 Near West Beach 2 Six 3 Yes, with a swimming pool 4 Yes 5 No, from March to October

Unit 12 (page 50)

1 1B 2D 3F 4E 5A 6C

2 1 Two euros and sixty-five cents 2 One/A hundred and one pounds 3 Five thousand, five hundred and fifty euros 4 Twenty-nine pounds and ninety-nine pence 5 Seventy-seven thousand euros 6 One/A million pounds

3 1 earn 2 check 3 spend 4 cost 5 save

4 1F desktop computer 2A hairdryer 3C camera 4B MP3 player 5E alarm clock 6D computer games

5 1 £12.99 2 China 3 cotton 4 wood 5 leather 6 plastic 7 glass 8 wool

6 1 chemist's 2 hairdresser's 3 bookshop 4 department store 5 travel agency 6 greengrocer's 7 bank 8 baker's

7 1 travel agency 2 greengrocer's 3 department store 4 bookshop 5 chemist's 6 hairdresser's 7 baker's 8 bank

8 1D 2C 3B 4A

9 1 Could 2 Would 3 Would 4 Could 5 Could 6 Do

Exam Practice (page 52)

R&W3 1A 2B 3C 4B

R&W7 1 was 2 a 3 me 4 them 5 still 6 very/really/ quite 7 it/ there 8 with 9 in 10 other

L5 (25) 1 cinema 2 £220 3 5 4 8.45 5 12(th)

S2 (26) 1 Airport Road, Newmarket 2 Yes, 200 3 Everything – fashion, furniture, sports, books, etc. 4 Yes, 20 cafés and 15 restaurants 5 10 p.m.

Answer key to the Skills & Vocab Maximiser

Unit 13 (page 54)

1 1 whale 2 giraffe 3 elephant 4 bear 5 dolphin 6 snake 7 tiger 8 monkey

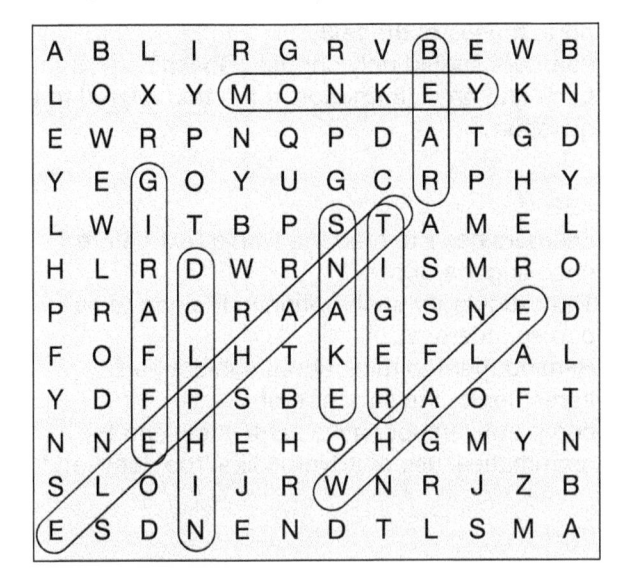

```
A B L I R G R V B E W B
L O X Y M O N K E Y K N
E W R P N Q P D A T G D
Y E G O Y U G C R P H Y
L W I T B P S T A M E L
H L R D W R N I S M R O
P R A O R A A G S N E D
F O F L H T K E F L A L
Y D F P S B E R A O F T
N N E H E H O H G M Y N
S L O I J R W N R J Z B
E S D N E N D T L S M A
```

2 (Suggested answers) 1 A, B, H 2 D, G, I, J 3 H 4 K 5 L 6 C 7 G, H, I, J, K 8 E 9 L 10 D, I, J

3 1 windy 2 icy 3 cloudy 4 snowy 5 wet 6 warm

4 1 north 2 south 3 east 4 west

5 1I 2K 3A 4J 5F 6L 7C 8B 9H 10G 11D 12E

6-7 Open answers

Exam Practice (page 56)

R&W5 1A 2B 3B 4B 5C 6C 7B 8C

R&W9 Sample answer

> My cat usually eats chicken or fish and always has some cat biscuits. You will need to feed him twice a day. Please can you play with him a little too.

L3 (27) 1B 2C 3B 4C 5C

S1 (28) 1 favourite animal 2 any pets 3 visiting zoos 4 on a farm 5 in the mountains... by the sea

Unit 14 (page 58)

1 1 angry 2 frightened/scared/afraid 3 happy 4 tired 5 sad 6 surprised

2 1 naughty 2 brave 3 friendly 4 funny 5 clever 6 popular

3 1K 2J 3I 4A 5G 6B 7L 8C 9H 10F 11E 12D

4 1 rich, poor 2 noisy, quiet 3 difficult, easy 4 hard, soft

5 1, 4, 5, 6, 8, 9, 10, 11, 12, 13, 14

6 1 receptionist 2 photographer 3 business woman 4 journalist 5 film star 6 taxi driver 7 cleaner 8 painter

7 1 photographer 2 taxi driver 3 receptionist 4 film star 5 cleaner

8 1A 2B 3C

9-10 Open answers

Exam Practice (page 60)

R&W5 1A 2C 3C 4B 5B

R&W7 1 when 2 could/can/should 3 in 4 the 5 gets/arrives 6 being 7 her 8 like/love 9 should 10 because

L4 (29) 1 28(th) 2 Ritherdon 3 6 4 station 5 blue (clothes)

S2 (30) 1 People who want to learn how to dance 2 Redwood Hall, High Street 3 Yes 4 Ballet, tap, hip-hop, latin, modern and others 5 No

Unit 15 (page 62)

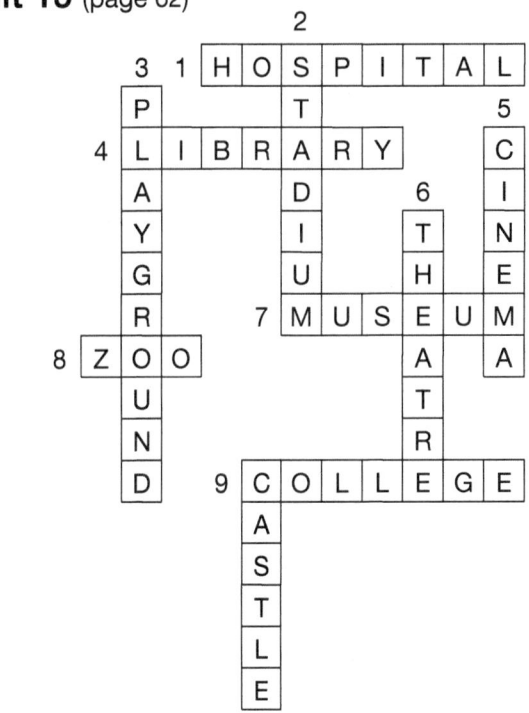

1

```
        2
   3  1 H O S P I T A L
      P   T           5
   4 L I B R A R Y    C
      A   D     6     I
      Y   I     T     N
      G   U     H     E
      R  7 M U S E U M
   8 Z O O      A     A
      U         T
      N         R
      D     9 C O L L E G E
            A
            S
            T
            L
            E
```

2 1C 2D 3A 4F 5B 6E

3 Open answers

4 1H 2D 3C 4B 5E 6F 7A 8G

5-6 Open answers

Exam Practice (page 64)

R&W1 1B 2G 3H 4E 5D

R&W8 1 £1 2 7 3 bridge 4 bus 5 umbrella

L1 (31) 1B 2B 3C

S1 (32) 1 this weekend 2 study at university 3 live in the city or the country 4 the theatre 5 museums

43

Guide to the Practice Tests

Reading and Writing

Part 1
Encourage learners to think about the main meaning of the notices before matching to sentences 1-5. They shouldn't just choose an answer because it contains the same word(s).
Remind learners not to use a letter more than once. Tell them to check their answers carefully at the end. They should look at the options they haven't chosen to make sure they don't fit sentences 1-5.
Tell them to make sure they don't choose the example notice.

Part 2
Remind learners that they need to check that the word fits grammatically as well. One of the words may be wrong because a preposition is missing or a different preposition is used, for example.
Tell learners to read the whole sentence with each word in it to see which one sounds best.

Part 3
<u>Questions 11-15</u>
Tell learners to read the question/statement very carefully and to focus on the type of response required, e.g. if the sentence is requesting permission, the response will need to give/refuse permission.
Remind learners to check that the response they choose fits the question or statement grammatically.

<u>Questions 16-20</u>
Remind learners to read the whole conversation through once to get a general understanding.
Tell them to check the option fits both with the sentences before and after it.
Remind learners to check that they have only used each option once, they haven't used the example again and that they are sure unused items do not fit anywhere.

Part 4
Remind learners to read the whole text to get a general understanding.
Tell them the 'Right' 'Wrong' answers are usually paraphrases of the text.
Learners should only choose 'Doesn't say' if they can't find any information in the text related to this question.

Part 5
Learners need to read the whole text before choosing the options.
They should try each option in the gap to see which one sounds best.
Remind them to think about subject-verb agreements, the structure of comparative/superlative sentences, and the grammatical use of adverbs like 'too' 'any' and 'yet'.

Part 6
Remind learners to count the number of spaces carefully and then to check they have written the correct number of letters.

Part 7
Tell learners to read the text once to get a general understanding.
They should read the text again when they have filled the gaps to make sure it makes sense.
Remind them to check their spelling.

Part 8
Remind learners to check they copy the words correctly.
Remind learners they do not have to write full sentences – one or two words is enough.

Part 9
Learners must check they have given the three pieces of information required.
Remind learners to check they have written at least 25 words and that it shouldn't be excessively over 35 words (inform learners that contracted verb forms, e.g. *doesn't*, count as two words).

Guide to the Practice Tests

Listening

Part 1
Learners must read the questions and look at the pictures carefully before listening.
They should use the second listening to check their answers.

Part 2
Tell learners to listen carefully for paraphrases of the options. It's unlikely exactly the same words will be used in the text.
Learners should also be aware that options may be wrong because the speaker decides to change his/her mind, or was unable to do option A so choose option C instead.

Part 3
Tell learners to read the questions carefully before listening.
Tell them not to worry if they can't understand every word. They only need to understand the main idea.

Parts 4 & 5
Tell learners they will only need to write one or two words for each question.
Remind them to check the spelling of months and days.
Tell them to listen carefully to numbers and letters. Is it 13 or 30? A or I?

Speaking

Part 1
Tell learners to answer the questions as fully as possible. One word answers are not enough.

Part 2
Remind learners to listen carefully to their partner's questions.
Remind learners that it doesn't matter if they make a few mistakes. The focus is on communication not accuracy, although candidates must be easily comprehensible.

Answer Key to the Practice Tests

Practice Test 1 (pages 66-79)

R&W1 1G 2F 3A 4E 5B
R&W2 6B 7C 8A 9C 10A
R&W3 11B 12C 13B 14A 15B 16H 17A 18E 19C 20G
R&W4 21A 22A 23B 24C 24A 25A 26B 27A
R&W5 28B 29C 30B 31C 32A 33A 34A 35C
R&W6 36 lift 37 luggage 38 passport 39 passenger 40 uniform
R&W7 41 for 42 your 43 with 44 has 45 about 46 but 47 It 48 me 49 the 50 one
R&W8 51 White Beach 52 6 p.m. 53 (the) station 54 bread 55 Owen
R&W9 Sample answer

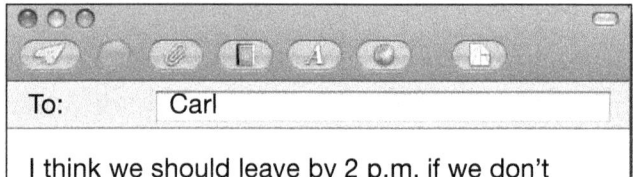

To: Carl

I think we should leave by 2 p.m. if we don't want to be late. Let's meet in front of the train station. Let's get some sandwiches to eat on the train.

See pages 57-59 for the recording scripts.

L1 (33) 1A 2C 3B 4C 5B
L2 (34) 6C 7H 8E 9G 10A
L3 (35) 11A 12A 13B 14C 15B
L4 (36) 16 April 17 hotel /room 18 15 19 30 20 money / cash
L5 (37) 21 Woolcott 22 explorer 23 4.30 24 school hall 25 18

Practice Test 2 (pages 80-93)

R&W1 1D 2F 3C 4A 5G
R&W2 6C 7B 8C 9C 10A
R&W3 11A 12B 13C 14A 15B 16G 17C 18E 19D 20B
R&W4 21A 22B 23C 24B 25C 26A 27A
R&W5 28C 29C 30A 31B 32C 33A 34B 35C
R&W6 36 towel 37 umbrella 38 ship 39 barbecue 40 octopus
R&W7 41 a 42 come/ go 43 I/ we 44 One 45 because 46 hour 47 was 48 for 49 have 50 me
R&W8 51 26 September 52 Mrs Jarvis 53 9 a.m. 54 food 55 team shirt
R&W9 Sample answer

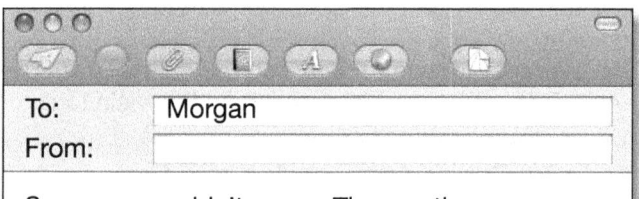

To: Morgan
From:

Sorry you couldn't come. The weather was very warm and sunny. We went to beach and did some windsurfing. We're going again in two weeks. Please come!

See pages 59-60 for the recording scripts.

L1 (38) 1A 2C 3A 4B 5C
L2 (39) 6G 7A 8C 9F 10B
L3 (40) 11B 12A 13A 14B 15C
L4 (41) 16 25(th)/ twenty fifth November 17 2.30/ half past two 18 5 19 Tyrone 20 465
L5 (42) 21 46 22 5th/ fifth 23 park 24 cinema 25 0307 912208

Recording Scripts

Recording scripts – Student's Book

(Class CD)

🎧 Unit 1 (page 11 ex. 15-16)

Teacher: Sarah, I'd like you to help me with the school magazine one day after school? Which day are you free?
Sarah: Well, on Monday I've got dancing at half past four.
Teacher: OK. What about Tuesday?
Sarah: I go to camera club. It's very good. My photos are much better now.
Teacher: And on Wednesday you have basketball practice. Is that right?
Sarah: I don't do that any more. I don't have time because I have to walk home from school with my brother and stay with him until my mum gets home.
Teacher: OK. So are you free on Thursday?
Sarah: Well, I usually go to the supermarket with my mum. She wants me to help her.
Teacher: And on Friday I suppose you go to the cinema or something like that.
Sarah: Actually, I have a piano lesson then. I don't go to the cinema much. I watch DVDs at home with my friends.
Teacher: What about the weekend? Are you busy on Saturday morning?
Sarah: I have to do extra work for my maths exam. A teacher comes to my house for an hour to help me.
Teacher: Oh dear. Maybe you can help me at lunch time instead.

🎧 Unit 2 (page 15 ex. 16-17)

1 Which woman is Clare's mother?
Boy: Is that your mum in the photo, Clare? The woman with the fair hair.
Girl: My mum doesn't have fair hair like me. Her hair's straight and dark.
Boy: Is that her?
Girl: That's my aunt. She has curly hair.

2 How old is David's brother?
Girl: Is your little brother eleven yet, David?
Boy: He's still only ten. His birthday is in July.
Girl: He's very tall. He looks twelve.
Boy: I know. Everyone thinks that.

3 Where is Olivia's dad?
Olivia: Are you still at work, Dad?
Dad: I finish early on Friday, remember? I'm at Grandma's house.
Olivia: Oh yes. Mum says dinner is at 8 o'clock.
Dad: That's fine. I want to get the 6.30 train home.

🎧 Unit 3 (page 19 ex. 15-16)

Grandmother: So how is your new school? Is it near your house?
Katie: Actually, it's too far to walk and you have to take three buses to get there so Mum drives me every day.
Grandmother: Do you have to leave the house early?
Katie: We don't leave until 8, so some days I don't get up until 7.30 and then I have my breakfast at about quarter to eight.
Grandmother: That's not too bad. Is your favourite subject still History?
Katie: I still like it but it's not my favourite subject. I love French and Spanish. I still hate Maths!
Grandmother: Maths was my favourite subject! What do you usually have for lunch?
Katie: The food is good. I'm usually too hungry for just a sandwich or a salad so I have pasta most days.
Grandmother: That's good. So you like your new school.
Katie: The teachers are very kind. But the building is very old and there isn't a pretty garden like in my old school.
Grandmother: Oh well. You can't have everything.

🎧 Exam Bank Units 1-3 (page 21)

Mark: Hi, Luke. I haven't got my weekly plan. What lessons do we have on Monday? Is the first lesson Maths?
Luke: That's right. At nine o'clock.
Mark: What's after that at ten o'clock? It's sport, isn't it?
Luke: Yes, but we haven't got football this week. It's hockey.
Mark: Oh no. I'm no good at that. I don't think I like Mondays! What's next, at eleven o'clock? I hope it isn't Science. I hate that.
Luke: That's on Tuesday. On Monday it's History.
Mark: Oh, that's OK. I don't mind that. Then it's lunch break. And what's after that, at 12.30?
Luke: We've got a grammar test on verbs, so don't forget to study for that.
Mark: It's a very bad day, isn't it? Then at 1.45 what have we got?
Luke: The last two lessons are OK. First it's Art – drawing pictures of our favourite sports stars.
Mark: Oh good. That sounds fun. What's next? Geography?
Luke: That's at 2.45. We have to finish drawing our maps of the river.
Mark: Oh, that's easy. Thanks, Luke.

🎧 Unit 4 (page 25 ex. 15-17)

Rebecca: Hello George. It's Rebecca. I want to ask you about your music lessons. Who's your teacher?
George: It's Mrs Quinlan. That's Q-U-I-N-L-A-N.
Rebecca: You're learning the keyboards, aren't you?
George: Yes, but she also teaches the guitar.
Rebecca: Oh, that's what I want to learn. How much are the lessons?
George: I pay £40 a month. So that's £10 for each lesson.
Rebecca: Right. That's OK. When does she teach?
George: She doesn't teach every day. She teaches on Thursday, Friday and Saturday.
Rebecca: That's fine for me. I'm busy on the other days. What's her phone number?
George: Wait a second. I'll give you her mobile number. OK. It's 0777 312456.
Rebecca: Where does she live?
George: She lives near the swimming pool. Her address is 27 Crichton Road. I'll spell that for you. It's C-R-I-C-H-T-O-N.
Rebecca: Oh, I know where that is. That's not too far to walk. Thanks, George.
George: That's OK…

47

🎧 Unit 5 (page 28 ex. 9-11)

1 Which sport does Alex like best?
Man: So is football still your favourite sport, Alex?
Alex: I still like it a lot but it isn't as much fun as skiing. I prefer that now.
Man: What about hockey? You play for the school team, don't you?
Alex: Yes, but I don't enjoy that very much.

2 Which sport does Laura want to learn?
Dad: Which sport do you want to do this year at the sports club?
Laura: Well, I'm tired of team sports like basketball. Can I play golf with you instead on Saturday mornings?
Dad: OK, but all your friends are playing baseball then.
Laura: I don't mind about that.

3 Which ticket does the man buy for the football match?
Man: I'd like to buy a 25-euro ticket, please, for the football match.
Woman: Sorry, there aren't any left. We've got the best seats at 42 euros.
Man: That's too expensive. Can I have one for 37 euros?
Woman: Let me check. Oh yes. There are a few of those left.

4 What time is swimming practice after school?
Mum: What time will you be home after swimming practice?
Girl: Not until six thirty.
Mum: That's very late.
Girl: Yes. We start later today, at 5.45 instead of 5.15.

🎧 Unit 6 (page 33 ex. 15-17)

Dad: Which restaurant do you want to go to for your birthday, Luke?
Luke: I like the Red Lion. We could go there.
Dad: But it gets very busy because so many people like it.
Luke: OK. What about the Little Kitchen? All my friends like Chinese food. And it doesn't cost much.
Dad: That's right! Or we can try The Happy Cook.
Luke: Can you sit outside there?
Dad: Yes. They have tables under the trees. It's lovely in summer.
Luke: But they don't do pizzas. That's what I like best.
Dad: Well, let's go to the Blue River. They do pizzas. But I can't hear what anyone is saying in there. It's so noisy.
Luke: Yes, but the bands they have are good.
Dad: There's also the Star Palace. That's a good place for large groups. They have lots of room.
Luke: Yes, and they do very good pizzas.
Dad: Or we can try The Castle. That opens this week.
Luke: Do they do pizza?

🎧 Exam Bank Units 4-6 (page 35)

Teacher: There's a swimming competition that I think you should enter, Olly.
Olly: Oh yes? What kind of competition, Mrs Lee?
Teacher: It's a competition to get into a new team. They want the best swimmers for the team.
Olly: That sounds good. Where is it?
Teacher: It's at the university pool.
Olly: That's quite far away. I don't know how to get there.
Teacher: Well, I can take you there in the school bus. There are some other pupils from the school going too.
Olly: And when is it? Not too soon, I hope.
Teacher: No, there's time to practise. It's on October 15th.
Olly: Right. And is it in the morning or the afternoon?
Teacher: It's in the afternoon at 2.30. And it finishes at 4.30.
Olly: Fine. That's not a problem. How old are the other swimmers?
Teacher: The team is for twelve to fifteen year olds. You're thirteen, aren't you? So that's good.
Olly: Yes.
Teacher: Ask your mum and dad about it and then phone me to tell me if you want to enter. My phone number is 454 6610.
Olly: OK. Thanks, Mrs Lee.

🎧 Unit 7 (page 39 ex. 18-20)

Kylie: Fred, can I ask you some questions about your trip to Kenya last year?
Fred: Sure, Kylie. What do you want to know?
Kylie: Well, is December a good time to go there?
Fred: I think it's probably the best time. April is good too. That's when I went, but don't go in June – it rains then.
Kylie: How long did you stay there?
Fred: I wanted to stay for a month, but I could only stay for three weeks. I think two weeks is too short if you want to see everything.
Kylie: OK. So did you stay in hotels all the time?
Fred: Actually, one of my mum's friends lives there and she invited me to stay with her. So I didn't have to camp!
Kylie: Right. Did you see lots of animals?
Fred: Yes! Lots! The giraffes were my favourite. We spent a long time looking for lions and elephants but we didn't see any.
Kylie: What's the best way to see the animals?
Fred: Well, most people go around in small buses. But my mum's friend drove me around, which was great. Next time I'd like to do a walking safari, on foot.
Kylie: That sounds a bit dangerous!

🎧 Unit 8 (page 43 ex. 14-18)

OK. Now, it's very important to follow these rules because they can help you to stay safe. So the first rule is that everyone has to wear a helmet. Right? The next thing to remember is that you can only use the skateboard park when there's an adult here. That's from 9 in the morning until 7 in the evening. Last week I caught some boys here at 10 p.m!

Also, this park isn't for young children. It's only for those who are 12 to 18, so please don't bring your younger sisters and brothers with you.

Another thing that you shouldn't bring with you is food, because you mustn't eat in the park. But drinks are OK.

When you're skateboarding you need to know who's behind you, so listening to music can be quite dangerous. It's really not a good idea. OK?

And one last thing. Please don't forget to bring £1.50 with you every time you use the park. Good! Any questions?

Recording Scripts

🔊12 Unit 9 (page 46 ex. 11-15)

Woman: Good morning. Can I help you?
Cathy: Hello. I'm looking for a party dress. My aunt is getting married next month. She's having a big party in the evening with a disco.
Woman: That sounds fun. Do you know what colour dress you'd like?
Cathy: Well, pink is my favourite colour but I already have a pink dress, so maybe green this time. But not yellow. I look terrible in that colour!
Woman: OK. Come and look at these…
Cathy: I like this one. It's very pretty. How much is it?
Woman: That one is now £80. It was £89, so there's nine pounds off the price.
Cathy: Mmm. That's quite expensive. Can I try it on, please?
Woman: Of course. Would you like to try some shoes with it? And I've got a bag that goes with that dress.
Cathy: I haven't got any shoes so I need to get some, but I've got lots of bags at home.
Woman: OK. It's summer so you don't need to wear tights… Oh, that looks lovely on you.
Cathy: I really like it but I think I need to show it to my mum. It's a very pretty colour and it feels very comfortable, so I hope she says yes.

🔊13 Exam Bank Units 7-9 (page 49)

1 How much is the jacket?
Man: How much is this jacket now?
Shop assistant: Well, it was £75 in the sale but we're taking another £20 off all the prices today.
Man: So it's £55, right? Down from £95.
Shop assistant: It's a very good price.

2 What does Sally want to buy?
Mum: What do you need to buy today, Sally?
Sally: I'd like to get some purple tights to go with my new purple leather gloves.
Mum: You need a belt too, don't you? You lost your other one.
Sally: No, it's OK. I found it again.

3 Where are Danny's trainers?
Danny: Mum, where are my trainers? I can't find them.
Mum: I hope you didn't leave them on the bus again.
Danny: No. I'm sure they're in the house somewhere.
Mum: Here they are. Under your bed. Put them in your bag. You've got football tomorrow.

🔊14 Unit 10 (page 53 ex. 13-14)

Owen: So you're coming to my house on Monday, aren't you, Archie?
Archie: Yeah, at lunch time.
Owen: OK. So in the afternoon we can go swimming at the pool, if you like.
Archie: Yes. I'm bringing my swimming things.
Owen: Good. Then on Tuesday, Dad's taking us to the museum. There's something on about dinosaurs at the moment.
Archie: That sounds quite interesting. And I've got two free tickets for the cinema. Would you like to go on Wednesday?

Owen: The new *Kid's Life* cartoon is out. That may be good.
Archie: OK.
Owen: Then on Thursday it's my friend Nathan's birthday. He isn't having a party but he wants us to go and play on his new computer game.
Archie: Cool. What about Friday?
Owen: Well, there's a music festival on in the park. Lots of reggae bands are playing. It's free.
Archie: Really? I hope it doesn't rain. And then Saturday's my last day. Shall we go skating?
Owen: Well, actually my grandma's having a barbecue for all the family. She wants us to go there for lunch.
Archie: OK. No problem. See you on Monday, then.

🔊15 Unit 11 (page 57 ex. 17-20)

Good morning everyone and welcome to Madingley Castle. My name's Gavin, that's G-A-V-I-N, and I'm your guide for today. Before we go into the castle itself, I want to show you the garden, as it's such a beautiful day. It's quite big so it'll take about an hour to walk around. Before lunch you have some free time and then at 1.30 please can everyone go to the shop? There are some tables outside where you can have your picnic. After lunch we're going to see the part of the castle where the children lived. You can see their bedrooms with all the old furniture. The only thing that's closed at the moment is the kitchen. So you can't see that, I'm afraid. The castle closes at 5.30 p.m. and your bus leaves at 5.45 from the car park. I think that's all the information you need… Oh, and if anyone would like a guidebook there's a special discount for students. You pay only £3.25 – normally it's £4.50. OK. Any questions?

Unit 12
🔊16 Vocabulary (page 58 ex. 3)

Man: How much does the camera cost?
Woman: We have a special price on at the moment. It's two hundred and ninety-six euros.

Boy: I want to save all my money to buy this DVD player. It costs eighty-seven dollars fifty.
Dad: That's a good idea.

Man: I'd like to pay for this radio, please.
Woman: That's fifty-nine pounds and ninety-nine pence. Are you paying by cash?

Girl: Can I get this electric toothbrush, Mum? It only costs twenty-three euros fifty.
Mum: That's too expensive.

Woman: There's a twenty percent discount on all TVs. This one's now only seven hundred and fifty pounds.
Man: That's not bad.

🔊17 Listening (page 59 ex. 9-10)

Amy: Hi, Clare. I love your bag. Is it new?
Clare: Yes. I bought it with some money my aunt gave me for my birthday.
Amy: I need to get a present for my mum. Was it expensive?
Clare: Not really. It was £13.50.
Amy: Oh, that's not bad. Is it OK if I buy one too?

49

Clare: Yeah, no problem.
Amy: Where did you get it?
Clare: At Mayhem.
Amy: I don't know that shop. How do you spell the name?
Clare: M-A-Y-H-E-M. They have things from all over the world. This bag is from Thailand. I also got these shoes from there. They're from India.
Amy: They're beautiful. Is it in the centre of town?
Clare: Yes. Walk from the station to the cinema. It's right next to it.
Amy: Oh, OK. I need to go there before Friday. That's my mum's birthday.
Clare: Well, don't go on Wednesday. It isn't open then.
Amy: OK. Thanks, Clare.

🎧 18 Exam Bank Units 10-12 (page 63)

Policeman: So what's the problem?
Martin: Someone has stolen my mobile phone.
Policeman: Where've you been this evening?
Martin: I've just come back from the football stadium. I went to see a band play there with some friends.
Policeman: So where do you think it was stolen?
Martin: Well, I was walking from the bus stop to my house. I went into a shop to buy a drink and I think it was taken there.
Policeman: Did you notice anyone acting strangely?
Martin: There was a boy who was also buying a drink but I'm sure it wasn't him. There was a young man standing close behind me. I think it was him because there wasn't anyone else except for the old man working in the shop!
Policeman: OK. How long have you had your phone?
Martin: I got it for my birthday. That was six months ago. I lost my last phone after only 9 months. I've now lost three phones.
Policeman: Oh dear! You need to look after your things more carefully. How much did it cost?
Martin: Was it £39 or £49? No. It was £49. I wanted one that cost £59, but my mum wouldn't buy it for me because I always lose them.
Policeman: No. Quite right!

🎧 19 Unit 13 (page 67 ex. 15-17)

1 What was the weather like yesterday?
  Man: It's good it's not raining again, like yesterday.
  Woman: Yes, it's nice and sunny now. But it's very cold.
  Man: I hope it doesn't snow.
  Woman: Me too!

2 Which animal has just arrived at the zoo?
  Mum: We're going to the zoo on Saturday.
  Boy: Oh good. I'd like to see the baby tiger again.
  Mum: Mmm. And there's a new polar bear. It's moved from Damforth zoo.
  Boy: I like those too, but it's a pity there aren't any lions at our zoo.

3 What has the girl just done?
  Dad: Have you taken the dog for a walk yet?
  Girl: I'm going to do that now. I've just finished having a game of ball with him in the garden.
  Dad: OK, but don't forget to brush him later.
  Girl: You've already told me to do that three times!

🎧 20 Unit 14 (page 71 ex. 19-21)

Lily: OK Grace, let's make a list of all our friends we need to buy presents for.
Grace: Alright, Lily. First there's Patrick.
Lily: Yes. Let's just get him some of his favourite sweets.
Grace: Yes. That's easy. What about Sarah?
Lily: We got her some chocolates last time. She liked those.
Grace: Well, let's get her a chocolate cake this time.
Lily: Fine. Jane likes sweet things too.
Grace: Mmm. Let's get her something different. Some nice soap, maybe.
Lily: OK. Nathan always likes books.
Grace: But that's a bit boring. I've seen a poster of his favourite singer. He'd like that.
Lily: Or a CD maybe.
Grace: He's already got so many of those.
Lily: OK. You're right. What about Rosie? She likes music too.
Grace: But we don't know which CDs she's already got.
Lily: I know. She loves Katy Allen. What about a T-shirt with a picture of her on it?
Grace: Yes. That's a nice idea. So now it's just Darius. What will we get him?
Lily: He likes cooking. Let's get him a book about cakes.
Grace: Perfect!

🎧 21 Unit 15 (page 75 ex. 17-19)

1 Which woman is Polly's Grandmother?
  Girl: Oh! There's my Grandma.
  Man: Which one is she? The one getting off the bus?
  Girl: That's her friend. They've just been shopping. My grandma gets off at the next stop.
  Man: Their shopping bags look very heavy.

2 Where is the man going to live?
  Woman: Are you going to get a house near your new office in the city?
  Man: I'd like to but it's too expensive so I'm going to stay here.
  Woman: Mmm, that's probably best. Or what about looking for a house in a village?
  Man: No. I like to have a few shops and restaurants nearby. And it's easy to get to the city by train.

3 Which is Edward's home?
  Woman: Do you have a big garden, Edward?
  Boy: Not any more. Before I lived in a house with a big garden and I miss that. But we do have a roof garden so it's OK.
  Woman: How nice.
  Boy: Yes. Much better than a balcony.

4 Where is it going to rain?
  Presenter: Tomorrow it'll be sunny everywhere in the morning but that's going to change in the afternoon in the east, where it will be very wet. The south will stay dry and warm and it's going to be sunny but quite windy in the west.

5 Where is the library?
  Man: OK, you need to come out of the station onto Mill Street. You'll see the library right in front of you on the other side of the road.

Recording Scripts

🎧22 Exam Bank Units 13-15 (page 77)

So now I want to tell you about your trip to Shepstow Zoo on Wednesday. You need to arrive at school by 8.30 so that we're all on the bus ready to leave at 8.45. Please don't be late. It'll take about one hour to get to the zoo. When you arrive you'll meet your guide for the day. He's called Angus Keeler, that's K-double E-L-E-R, and he will take you to meet some of the animals. It'll be very exciting because he'll be able to show you the newest member of the zoo, born only four weeks ago. His name's Chulu and he's a lion. You won't be able to take photos of Chulu yet because his mum won't like it, but you can buy a photo of him to take home for £2.50. You can take photos of the other animals, of course, so don't forget to bring your cameras. One thing you mustn't use in the zoo is your mobile phone, so I think it's best for you to leave these at home. OK. Any questions?

COMMUNICATION BANK

🎧23 Communication Bank 1
(page 93 ex. 1-2)

Jim: Hello. Welcome to City Basketball Club. My name's Jim. What's your name?
Marcus: My name's Marcus.
Jim: And what's your surname, Marcus?
Marcus: It's Bowling.
Jim: How do you spell that?
Marcus: B-O-W-L-I-N-G
Jim: Great. Oh yes, I can see your name on the list of new players. OK. How old are you, Marcus?
Marcus: I'm twelve.
Jim: Fine. The other new boys are the same age as you, so that's good. And what school do you go to?
Marcus: I go to North London College.
Jim: Oh yes. We have some other players from your school at this club. And one last question. Where do you live?
Marcus: Flat 51, Acland House, Barnet Road.
Jim: Do you spell that A-C-K?
Marcus: No, it's A-C-L-A-N-D.
Jim: Good. I think that's all the information I need. So what…

🎧24 Communication Bank 1 (page 93 ex. 4)

1 I live in York Road. That's Y-O-R-K.
2 Her address is Eccleston House, 4 High Street, Southampton. You spell Eccleston, E-C-C-L-E-S-T-O-N.
3 You must get off the train in Swansea. That's S-W-A-N-S-E-A.
4 You spell it C-A-M-B-R-I-D-G-E. Don't forget to send me a postcard!
5 Every year there is a festival in Edinburgh, in Scotland. That's E-D-I-N-B-U-R-G-H.

🎧25 Communication Bank 2
(pages 93-94 ex. 1-2)

Mrs Simpson: Hello, Rachel. I'm phoning about the volleyball match next week.
Rachel: Oh, yes. What date is that?
Mrs Simpson: It's on Tuesday.
Rachel: That's the 22nd, isn't it?
Mrs Simpson: Yes. It's in the afternoon at 2.30.
Rachel: Sorry, I can't hear you very well. What time?
Mrs Simpson: 2.30, but we have to be there at 2 o'clock.
Rachel: OK. And which school is it at?
Mrs Simpson: Arkesden school. A-R-K-E-S-D-E-N.
Rachel: Sorry, Could you spell that again, please?
Mrs Simpson: A-R-K-E-S-D-E-N. It's in Redbridge.
Rachel: Oh. That's a long way. So we need to go by bus.
Mrs Simpson: Yes. The bus leaves at 1 o'clock from the library, so we must all meet there at 12.45.
Rachel: OK. Do I need to bring anything?
Mrs Simpson: You need to bring £5.50 for the bus.
Rachel: How much? £5.15 or £5.50?
Mrs Simpson: £5.50. OK? So see you on Tuesday. Bye.

🎧26 Communication Bank 3 (page 94 ex. 1)

Ruth: What are you doing on Saturday evening?
Lauren: I'm not sure. Why?
Ruth: Would you like to come to my house to watch the dance competition on TV?
Lauren: Yes, I'd love to. What time shall I come?
Ruth: At 6.30. Shall I ask Erin too?
Lauren: I think she may be at her aunt's house.
Ruth: I'll ask her tomorrow. What about food? Shall we get some pizzas?
Lauren: That's a good idea. I'll bring a cake.
Ruth: OK. Great.
Lauren: See you on Saturday.
Ruth: Bye.

🎧27 Communication Bank 4
(page 95 ex. 1-2)

1 What time does Madeleine have to arrive at school?
Simon: So what time do you have to be at school, Madeleine?
Madeleine: Our lessons start at ten to nine but we have to be there before that – by eight thirty-five.
Simon: How long does it take to walk to school?
Madeleine: Only fifteen minutes, so I leave the house at twenty past eight.

2 What can the boys do in the library?
Dan: Can we eat our sandwiches in here, Miss, while we do our homework?
Miss Miller: Boys, you know you mustn't bring food into the library – you can only bring bottles of water.
Dan: And we can't listen to music either.
Miss Miller: That's right. And remember, no talking.
Dan: OK, Miss.

3 Why can't the boy go to his piano lesson?
Peter: I'm afraid I can't come to my piano lesson again this week.
Mrs Giles: What's the problem, Peter? Your hand is OK now, I hope.
Peter: Yes, it's fine now, thank you, but I have to leave school early to go to the dentist. I'm very sorry.
Mrs Giles: That's a pity, Peter. You need to practise a lot for your piano exam next month.

🎧 28 (page 96 ex. 5)

1 **A** I'm sorry I can't go to your party.
   B What a pity!
2 **A** I'm sorry I'm late.
   B It doesn't matter.
3 **A** I'm afraid I don't know the answer.
   B Don't worry about it.
4 **A** I'm afraid I can't play tennis with you today.
   B Oh dear!

🎧 29 Communication Bank 5 (page 96 ex. 1)

Jon: That's a cool bag.
Steve: Thanks very much. I really like it too.
Jon: Where's it from?
Steve: I think it's from a shop in London.
Jon: Who gave it to you?
Steve: My brother gave it to me for my birthday.
Jon: Did he give you that scarf too?
Steve: No, I bought that in a market last month.

🎧 30 Communication Bank 6
(page 96 ex. 1-2)

1 **A:** Could you bring me the menu, please?
   B: Of course, sir.
2 **A:** Do you mind if I sit here?
   B: Not at all.
3 **A:** Could you help me with my bag, please?
   B: Yes, certainly.
4 **A:** Could you talk more quietly, please?
   B: Yes. Sorry.
5 **A:** Can I borrow six books?
   B: Sorry, you can only take four.
6 **A:** Do you mind if I close the door?
   B: No, I don't mind.
7 **A:** Could we have the bill, please?
   B: Just a moment, please.
8 **A:** Could I see your ticket, please?
   B: Yes. Here you are.

🎧 31 Communication Bank 7
(page 97 ex. 1-2)

Charlotte: I hate getting up when it's dark and cold but I don't mind walking to school in the snow. I don't like being in school when it's a lovely sunny day. I'd prefer to be outside in the park. My favourite kind of days are in the autumn when the sun is shining and the leaves are falling. I think those days are really special. I try to catch the leaves with my dog. My worst kind of day is when it's raining and there's nothing to do. It makes me feel sad.

🎧 32 Communication Bank 8
(page 98 ex. 1-2)

1 **When did the boy's grandfather first get a car?**
   Derren: When did you get your first car, Grandad?
   Grandad: Let's see. A long time ago. I could drive when I was 17 – my dad taught me. So that was in 1959. But I wasn't able to get a car until a few years later.
   Derren: Why not?
   Grandad: We didn't have enough money. I didn't get the car until 1965, two years after I left college in 1963.

2 **What could Rob's sister do when she was ten?**
   Sophie: Is that your sister Ellie in the photo, Rob?
   Rob: Yes. She was only ten then but she could ride better than anybody in her school.
   Sophie: Does she still ride?
   Rob: Now she's into racing bikes. She's really fast. Faster than me. But I'm better at sailing than her.

3 **What couldn't the girl do last night?**
   Elena: I'm afraid I couldn't do all my science homework last night, Miss.
   Miss Edwards: Why not? Weren't you able to find the information on the Internet?
   Elena: Yes, I was. And I was able to do the drawing of a flower, but I forgot to take my science book home so I couldn't do the reading.
   Miss Edwards: Well, you must do it tonight. OK?

🎧 33 Communication Bank 9
(page 99 ex. 1-2)

1 **Does Sheila think it will rain later?**
   Andrew: Shall we have a barbecue later, Sheila?
   Sheila: I'm not sure that's such a good idea.
   Andrew: Why not?
   Sheila: There may be a storm this evening.

2 **Does George think he will win the race?**
   Katherine: How do you think you will do in the race?
   George: I won my last two races but this one may be different.
   Katherine: But everyone thinks you'll win again this time.
   George: Well, I hope I do but I can't say I'm certain.

3 **Does Nigel think he will be a doctor?**
   Mrs Tomlins: So do you want to be a doctor when you grow up, like your dad?
   Nigel: Of course it's a really good thing to be a doctor, but I've already decided I won't study medicine at university.
   Mrs Tomlins: What does your father think about that?
   Nigel: Oh, he doesn't mind. He hopes I'll be a writer.

🎧 34 Communication Bank 10
(page 100 ex. 1-2)

1 OK, so to get to my house walk as far as the traffic lights. You'll see the petrol station on your right. Turn left at the lights and walk straight down Brook Road.

2 There is a quick way to get to my house through the park but it's easy to get lost, so walk past the park and cross the road when you get to the end.

3 I live down that road. When you come to the Chinese restaurant, you'll see my apartment building on the opposite side of the road next to a newsagent's.

Recording Scripts

Recording scripts – Skills & Vocab Maximiser

(Audio CD-ROM)

🎧 Unit 1 (page 7 ex. 8)

1. 21 April
2. 1998
3. 9.00 a.m.
4. 2009
5. 12.10 p.m.
6. 101 Bridge Street
7. 3.45 p.m.
8. 1 November 2001
9. 19 June 2010
10. 2.30 a.m.

🎧 Unit 1 Listening Exam Practice (page 11)

1 What time does the boy have breakfast at the weekend?
Girl: Do you get up late at the weekend?
Boy: Mmm. I get up at about 8 o'clock at the weekend.
Girl: What do you have for breakfast?
Boy: My family always eats together at the weekend. But we have to eat quite early, at quarter past eight, because my brother and I play football at 9.30.

2 What does the girl do on Saturday mornings?
Boy: Do you go shopping with your friends on Saturday morning?
Girl: I can't in the morning because I have to go to the park with my dog. And in the afternoon I have a dance class.
Boy: So no time for shopping.
Girl: I know. It's terrible.

3 When is the girl's birthday?
Boy: When's your birthday? Is it the 20th of July?
Girl: That's my mum's birthday. Mine is on the 24th.
Boy: When's your party?
Girl: On the 22nd because that's a Saturday.

🎧 Unit 1 Speaking Exam Practice (page 11)

1. What time do you get up at the weekend?
2. What do you have for breakfast?
3. What do you do on Saturday mornings?
4. When is your birthday?

🎧 Unit 2 Listening Exam Practice (page 13)

Girl: Grandma, can I ask you some questions? It's for my homework.
Grandma: Yes. Of course, Zadie. What do you want to know?
Girl: Well, first of all your name. Your first name is Gwendolyn, isn't it?
Grandma: Yes. That's right. Do you know how to spell it? G-W-E-N-D-O-L-Y-N.
Girl: Alright. What's your surname? It's different surname to Grandpa's, isn't it?
Grandma: Yes. It's Morrissey.
Girl: How do you spell that?
Grandma: M-O-double R-I-double S-E-Y.
Girl: OK. And when were you born?
Grandma: A long time ago! I'm 67 now.
Girl: That's not so old. My friend's Grandmother is 83.
Grandma: Well, I feel old sometimes.
Girl: You weren't born in the UK, were you?
Grandma: No, I wasn't. I was born in Sydney in Australia. I moved here after I met Grandpa.
Girl: What about your family? How many brothers and sisters have you got?
Grandma: I come from a big family. I've got five – three brothers and two sisters.
Girl: That's a lot.
Grandma: Yes. I've got two brothers still in Australia. You don't know them.
Girl: I'd like to meet them one day. Now. Just one more question.
Grandma: What's that?
Girl: What's your favourite colour?
Grandma: That's easy, It's green.
Girl: Mine's blue.

🎧 Unit 2 Speaking Exam Practice (page 13)

1. What's your surname?
2. How do you spell that?
3. How old are you?
4. Where were you born?
5. How many brothers and sisters have you got?
6. What's your favourite colour?

🎧 Unit 3 Listening Exam Practice (page 17)

Conor: I've got a lot of homework to do this weekend, Mum.
Mum: Oh dear, Conor. What do you have to do?
Conor: Well, for Business Studies I have to read 20 pages of my book.
Mum: That's a lot.
Conor: Yes. And then there's Computer Studies. We've got some exercises to do in our textbook.
Mum: What else? Do you have any English homework?
Conor: Yes. The teacher wants us to check the letters we wrote in class and write them again. This time without any mistakes.
Mum: Well, I can help you with that. And what about French?
Conor: I have to learn all the words in my vocabulary notebook for a spelling test on Monday.
Mum: Oh well. You're good at foreign languages. That's not so difficult.
Conor: Mmm. Maths is OK because we just have to play some games on a Maths website.

53

Mum: That's good. Is that all?
Conor: No. There's Science too. We have to draw a picture of a plant and label it.
Mum: What a busy weekend!

🎧 8 Unit 3 Speaking Exam Practice (page 17)

1 Is the competition for all ages?
2 What do you have to write?
3 How much must you write?
4 When is the closing date?
5 Is there a prize?

🎧 9 Unit 4 Listening Exam Practice (page 21)

Grandad: I hear you're doing a photography course now, Lewis.
Lewis: That's right, Grandad.
Grandad: When are the lessons?
Lewis: They're after school on Wednesdays, Thursdays and Fridays. I go to the one on Fridays, but I want to change to Wednesdays because my friend goes to that one.
Grandad: Do you like it?
Lewis: It's fun but it's quite difficult and my teacher does everything very fast.
Grandad: Do you have to pay for the lessons?
Lewis: Yes, they're £5 each and then you have to pay £6.00 for a pack of photography paper. And I'm using a school camera and that costs £10 per term.
Grandad: That's quite a lot, isn't it? How many students are there in the class?
Lewis: Only 12. But all different ages. From 13 to 17.
Grandad: That's nice. What do you like taking photographs of?
Lewis: People doing things like football or running, not my family or people in the street.
Grandad: Can you choose what type of photographs to take?
Lewis: No. Every week it's different. It's buildings this week. Last week it was animals and we're doing flowers the week after.
Grandad: It sounds very interesting.

🎧 10 Unit 4 Speaking Exam Practice (page 21)

1 What do you learn on the art course?
2 What date does it start?
3 Where is the course?
4 Is the course for everyone?
5 How can I get more information?

🎧 11 Unit 5 Listening Exam Practice (page 25)

OK. Can you all listen carefully now? I'm going to give you some information about the hockey match on Saturday. The school bus is going to take us there but your parents need to bring you home. So when you get to school, come straight to the school playground – I'll wait for you there. Don't go to the school office. The match is at ten o'clock so we need to leave school at 8.45. So make sure you arrive in school by 8.30. Don't be late because we will have trouble getting there on time. The match is against Oakham School in Dunmow. That's O-A-K-H-A-M – make sure your parents know where it is. Your parents need to get there by 11.30. Tell your parents it's easy to park near the school. I'm afraid the school car park is closed at weekends. So the best place is in the supermarket. There's always lots of space there. If you have any problems you can call me on 0998765234. That's my mobile number. Now has anybody got anything to say...

🎧 12 Unit 5 Speaking Exam Practice (page 25)

1 What's the name of the swimming pool?
2 Is the swimming pool big?
3 Is there a pool outside?
4 What lessons do they do?
5 Where is the swimming pool?

🎧 13 Unit 6 Listening Exam Practice (page 29)

1 **What does the girl decide to have for lunch?**
Girl: Mum, can I have a pizza for lunch?
Mum: Sorry. There aren't any left. Why don't you have a salad?
Girl: I feel like something hot. I suppose I'll have soup.
Mum: OK. We've got tomato or carrot.

2 **What's the boy's favourite food?**
Girl: Is there anything you like on the menu, Tom?
Tom: There's pasta. I like that. But they haven't got steak.
Girl: Is that what you like best?
Tom: Yes. But I can have a burger instead.

3 **How much does the ice cream cost?**
Jamie: This ice cream looks very good.
Girl: But look how much it costs, Jamie. I usually pay £1.20 in our shop. Here it's £1.99.
Jamie: That's OK. I've got enough money. I've got £2.50.
Girl: I don't want one anyway. It's too cold today.

🎧 14 Unit 6 Speaking Exam Practice (page 29)

1 Do you like cooking?
2 What can you cook?
3 Do you learn to cook at school?
4 Who's the best cook in your family?
5 Do you prefer home cooking or restaurant food?

🎧 15 Unit 7 Listening Exam Practice (page 33)

Mum: So what did you do on your school trip, Liam?
Liam: It was great. We really enjoyed ourselves. We did something different every day. We arrived on Friday afternoon and went for a 5-kilometre walk in the woods. We found lots of small animals and insects.

Recording Scripts

Mum: What did you do on Saturday?
Liam: It wasn't windy enough to go sailing so we rode bicycles around the lake instead.
Mum: That sounds fun. What about Sunday?
Liam: We spent the day on the lake. I caught a big fish. We cooked it on the fire in the evening.
Mum: Really? I'm sure that was nice. Where did you go on Monday?
Liam: There was a thunderstorm that day so we stayed inside and played games. I learnt how to play table tennis. It's fun.
Mum: Was the weather OK on Tuesday?
Liam: Yes. It was a nice day so some people went swimming but a group of us did windsurfing instead.
Mum: Oh. And what did you do on your last day?
Liam: On Wednesday we learnt how to climb. Now I know how to do it safely.
Mum: Oh that's good, but perhaps I didn't want to know that.

🎧 16 Unit 7 Speaking Exam Practice (page 33)
1 What's the name of the campsite?
2 Does it close in the winter?
3 Can you buy food there?
4 Is it a big campsite?
5 How far is it from the beach?

🎧 17 Unit 8 Listening Exam Practice (page 37)
Auntie Lizzie: Hello, Robert. How are you?
Robert: Much better thanks, Auntie Lizzie.
Auntie Lizzie: So when was the accident?
Robert: On Thursday – not yesterday, last week.
Auntie Lizzie: I can see you've hurt your eye and your arms and legs.
Robert: Yes. I'm lucky it was only my nose that's broken. But my leg still hurts a lot.
Auntie Lizzie: So were you in the skate park when this happened?
Robert: I was on my way there. I was only around the corner from home, in the next road.
Auntie Lizzie: Did anyone phone for an ambulance?
Robert: A nice woman looked out from her window. She came out and drove me to the hospital. So I didn't need to phone for an ambulance or a taxi.
Auntie Lizzie: That was lucky. So how long were you in hospital?
Robert: Well, it was late in the evening when I saw the doctor and he said I couldn't go home until the morning.
Auntie Lizzie: So where's your skateboard now?
Robert: No one knows. When my friends went to look for it they couldn't find it. It doesn't matter because I'm sure it was broken.
Auntie Lizzie: Well, you certainly don't need it at the moment.

🎧 18 Unit 8 Speaking Exam Practice (page 37)
1 Do you get colds easily?
2 What do you do to stay healthy?
3 Do you get enough sleep?
4 How often do you miss school?
5 How much sport do you do?
6 Do you enjoy doing dangerous activities like skateboarding

🎧 19 Unit 9 Listening Exam Practice (page 41)
Hi Sam. It's Anthony. You said it would be OK for you to get my team football shirt when you get yours. Mrs Jackson says the best place to buy the shirts is a shop called Number One. It's bigger than the one in the shopping centre and cheaper. The address is 330 Wycliffe Street. That's W-Y-C-L-I-F-F-E. I think it's quite easy to find. Remember the team colour is different now so we need to get dark green shirts, not light green ones. Mrs Jackson says the shirts are often too big so we all only need small. Medium will be too big. I can give you the money when I see you if that's OK. Mrs Jackson says they should be $22.99 but she didn't think we could get a discount. Don't forget we have our first match on Saturday so you need to get them before then. Let me know if you have any problems. Thanks Sam.

🎧 20 Unit 9 Speaking Exam Practice (page 41)
1 What's the name of the shop?
2 Where is it?
3 What does it sell?
4 When does the sale start?
5 What time does it open and what time does it close?

🎧 21 Unit 10 Listening Exam Practice (page 45)
1 **Which programme is Grandad watching?**
   Boy: Can I watch cartoons now?
   Mum: Sorry, Grandad's watching TV.
   Boy: Well, the football match is on soon.
   Mum: You can watch that when the news finishes.

2 **What does Patrick want to buy for his dad?**
   Patrick: Look, Mum. This is a book about dad's favourite tennis player
   Mum: Do you want to get it as a present for him, Patrick?
   Patrick: That's a good idea. I read about this book in a magazine. There was a free poster of him in it.
   Mum: Well, I'll buy this for him now and you can give me the money later.

3 **What is Ellie doing on Saturday evening?**
   Dad: Are you going to a party on Saturday, Ellie?
   Ellie: Not this Saturday. I'm staying in. There's a TV show I want to watch. Sally's coming over to watch it with me.
   Dad: What about studying for your test?
   Ellie: I'm doing that on Sunday.

(22) Unit 10 Speaking Exam Practice (page 45)
1 What type of TV programmes do you enjoy watching?
2 Who's your favourite actor?
3 How often do you go to the cinema?
4 What's your favourite film and why do you like it?

(23) Unit 11 Listening Exam Practice (page 49)
Boy: Mum, have you seen my glasses?
Mum: I think they're in the hall.
Boy: Oh yes. On the desk. Found them. What about my school bag?
Mum: Isn't that in your bedroom?
Boy: I've looked there. It isn't in the cupboard.
Mum: Well, look under the bed. That's where it was last time.
Boy: OK. Yes you're right.
Mum: Have you got your sports shoes?
Boy: Yes. They were on the stairs so I put them in the car so I wouldn't forget them today.
Mum: Well done. And have you got your key? I'll be out when you get home.
Boy: I put it on the bottom shelf in the bathroom last night.
Mum: And I moved it to the kitchen table. It should still be there.
Boy: OK. Yes. Got it.
Mum: It's cold today. You need gloves. Get them out of the cupboard.
Boy: In the hall?
Mum: In your bedroom.
Boy: Oh, OK.
Mum: And don't forget your phone.
Boy: Is it on the kitchen table?
Mum: I can't see it there. When did you last have it?
Boy: I phoned Luke while I was watching TV.
Mum: Here it is. Under your jacket on the sofa.

(24) Unit 11 Speaking Exam Practice (page 49)
1 Where is the house?
2 How many bedrooms does it have?
3 Does it have a nice garden?
4 Is there a TV?
5 Can you rent it all year?

(25) Unit 12 Listening Exam Practice (page 53)
The Computer Store sale starts tomorrow. Choose from hundreds of different computers all at our best ever prices.
Come and find us at number 10 Lomax Street just next door to the cinema. But you'll have to be quick. We've got some of our best-selling laptops at impossibly low prices. You can get a fantastic new laptop for just £220, down from £430. But there are only fifty on sale at this very special price so don't delay.
And what's more – if you're at school or college you can get an extra 5 per cent off that price again. How good is that?!
As usual our friendly staff are here with all the help and information you need. So make sure you get here early when the doors open tomorrow at 8.45. The Computer Store sale starts tomorrow, December 8th and ends on the 12th December. Don't miss it!

(26) Unit 12 Speaking Exam Practice (page 53)
1 Where is the shopping centre?
2 Does it have a lot of shops?
3 What can you buy there?
4 Is there anywhere to eat?
5 What time does it close?

(27) Unit 13 Listening Exam Practice (page 57)
Girl: I'm thinking of going on the mountain adventure trip next year. You went last year, Steven, didn't you? Do you think I'd like it?
Steven: Yes. It was great. The cycling was the most fun but some of the walks were really beautiful. The rock climbing was hard.
Girl: How many students went?
Steven: It was a bigger group than usual. Forty wanted to go but there was only space for thirty. Twenty would be best.
Girl: How long were you away?
Steven: Two weeks, but the teachers think that's too long. The last four days everyone was very tired, So next year it'll only be ten days.
Girl: Did you have good weather?
Steven: Well, it was very cold but we were lucky because it can be foggy and wet even in summer.
Girl: Did you have the right clothes?
Steven: Yes. I had a warm jacket but my hands were like ice because I didn't have any gloves. I was glad my mum made me take my ski hat.
Girl: I must remember that. What about money?
Steven: Well all food was included and there weren't any shops to buy presents but there are some extra things you can do, like horse-riding, and you need to pay for those.

(28) Unit 13 Speaking Exam Practice (page 57)
1 What's your favourite animal? Why do you like them?
2 Do you have any pets?
3 Do you like visiting zoos?
4 Would you like to live on a farm? Why?/ Why not?
5 Would you prefer to spend a holiday in the mountains or by the sea?

(29) Unit 14 Listening Exam Practice (page 61)
Rachel: Hi, Katy, it's Rachel. I just wanted to tell you you're invited to Lorna's party. She's lost your phone number.
Katy: Oh. When is it?
Rachel: It's next Saturday – not this one – it's on October the 28th.
Katy: That's fine. I'm not doing anything then. Where's she having the party?

Recording Scripts

Rachel: She's not having it at home. It's at the sports club on Ritherdon Road.
Katy: Which road?
Rachel: Ritherdon. That's R-I-T-H-E-R-D-O-N.
Katy: Oh. I've never been there before. What time does it start?
Rachel: We need to be there for 6 and it finishes at 10.
Katy: OK. Can I come with you – because I don't know where it is?
Rachel: Yes. I'm going on the underground, so I'll see you in front of the station at 5.30. My dad will collect us after the party.
Katy: Great. Thanks. Oh! Do I need to wear anything special?
Rachel: Oh yes. I nearly forgot. She wants everyone to wear blue clothes. Everything's going to be that colour – even the food!
Katy: Sounds interesting. Well thanks very much Rachel…

(30) Unit 14 Speaking Exam Practice (page 61)

1 Who is the notice for?
2 Where is the academy?
3 Can you go there every day?
4 What styles of dancing can you learn?
5 Does it cost anything the first time?

(31) Unit 15 Listening Exam Practice (page 65)

1 What is Tom going to visit on his school trip?
Dad: Why aren't you wearing your uniform today, Tom?
Tom: I'm going on a trip. We're going to see where they make chocolate.
Dad: That sounds more interesting than going to a museum.
Tom: Yes, but I liked our last trip to the castle.

2 Where is the nearest bus stop?
Girl: You know where the nearest bus stop is, don't you?
Boy: Just outside the theatre.
Girl: That's a much longer walk. The one on the bridge is closer to her. And you get off in front of the library.
Boy: Oh, OK.

3 What time is the girl going to meet her dad?
Dad: So shall I collect you at six as usual?
Girl: Well, my dance lesson starts two hours later today.
Dad: So, at eight then.
Girl: Yes because it starts at seven.

(32) Unit 15 Speaking Exam Practice (page 65)

1 What are you going to do this weekend?
2 Are you going to study at university?
3 Would you prefer to live in the city or the country?
4 Do you ever go to the theatre?
5 Do you enjoy going to museums?

(33) Practice Test 1 Part 1 (page 74)

This is the Total KET Practice Test 1.
There are five parts to the test. Parts One, Two, Three, Four and Five. We will now stop for a moment before we start the test.
Please ask any questions now because you must NOT speak during the test.

Now look at the instructions for Part One.
You will hear five short conversations. You will hear each conversation twice. There is one question for each conversation. For each question, choose the right answer, A, B or C. Here is an example:
What time does the boy's football match start?
Dad: What time is your football match tomorrow, Isaac?
Issac: I don't think it's until ten, because we're meeting at school at nine o'clock
Dad: And it takes about half an hour to get there.
Issac: Yes, and we'll need time to get ready.

Now listen again

The answer is 10 o'clock so there is a tick in box A. Now we are ready to start.

1 What will the weather be like tomorrow?
Girl: Can we go to the beach tomorrow Dad?
Dad: I don't think it'll be as sunny as today. They said so on the radio.
Girl: It's just going to be cloudy. That's OK.
Dad: Yes. It'll stay dry and warm all day.

Now listen again

2 What did the girl have for lunch?
Girl: When's dinner? I'm so hungry.
Mum: Not until later. You need to eat more at lunchtime. A sandwich isn't enough.
Girl: I had soup today because I was cold. And I sometimes have a salad.
Mum: You should have a hot meal every day.

Now listen again

3 How will the boy get home from his friend's house?
Mum: How are you getting back from Stan's house, Eddie?
Eddie: I'll take my bike.
Mum: I don't think that's a good idea. It'll be dark. Can you take the bus? I can't come and get you because Dad's got the car and he won't be back in time.
Eddie: OK, Mum.

Now listen again

4 Which tickets do they decide to get for the concert?
Brian: Hi Polly. It's Brian. Do you want me to get you a ticket for The Cats? It's on the 18th December. They're either £25, £35, or £45.
Polly: The cheapest seats are terrible! Let's get the most expensive ones. I want to be at the front.
Brian: I think you're right. Ok I'll book them now.

Now listen again

57

5 What has the girl bought for her mother?
Girl: Look what I got for mum. Do you think she'll like them?
Boy: They're really nice. She lost her last pair of gloves, didn't she?
Girl: Yes. She's got a scarf in the same colour.
Boy: Great! I could get her a hat to go with them.

Now listen again

This is the end of Part One. Now look at Part Two.

🎧 Practice Test 1 Part 2 (page 75)

Listen to Tyler talking to his mum about an arts festival at school.
What activity did each person do?
For questions 6-10, write a letter A-H next to each person.
You will hear the conversation twice.

Mum: What did you do at the school arts festival, Tyler?
Tyler: I did photography.
Mum: Oh? Did Seth do that too?
Tyler: He's already done a photography course so he did the cartoon activity. He's really good at art.
Mum: What about Kirsty? She's good at art too, isn't she?
Tyler: Yes but she doesn't like painting animals so she did the singing course instead.
Mum: Did anyone do any dancing?
Tyler: Yes. Conor. He likes Indian films and music so he wanted to try the dancing. He was the only boy so they let him play the drums, too while the girls danced.
Mum: Jasmina can do Indian dancing, can't she?
Tyler: Yes. She's very good. The teacher told her it would be too easy, so she did Scottish country dancing.
Mum: And how about Brad?
Tyler: Well, he chose Computer art but that was full so the teacher asked him to do Animal painting. I told him to do the drums but he didn't like that idea.
Mum: It sounds like you all had a fantastic day.

Now listen again

This is the end of Part Two. Now look at Part Three.

🎧 Practice Test 1 Part 3 (page 76)

Listen to Josie talking to her dad about her birthday party. For each question, choose the right answer (A, B or C). You will hear each conversation twice.

Dad: We need to decide the date for your party, Josie.
Josie: Well, the 7th isn't a Saturday. And lots of people will be on holiday on the 10th, so the 3rd of July is best.
Dad: OK. How many do you want to invite?
Josie: Not the whole year group – that's 75... 40 is enough. Becky had 55 at her party but that was too many.

Dad: Fine. Where are we going to have it? At home?
Josie: Yes. We can use the garden. The sports club's too big and the village hall isn't very nice.
Dad: Yes. I think you're right – but it can't finish too late.
Josie: Is half past ten OK? Ten's a bit early and some parents will think eleven is too late.
Dad: Yes. I agree. Do you want people to wear anything special?
Josie: Mmmm. Like only black or white? I think everyone'll be more comfortable in jeans.
Dad: Now, I need to order a cake. What kind shall I get?
Josie: That's difficult! Coffee is my favourite but not everyone likes that so maybe strawberry this year. I had chocolate last year.
Dad: Good idea.

Now listen again

This is the end of Part Three. Now look at Part Four.

🎧 Practice Test 1 Part 4 (page 77)

You will hear a boy called Gareth asking a friend about a golf competition. Listen and complete each question. You will hear the conversation twice.

Boy 1: Are you going to enter the golf competition at Seaton Golf Club, Gareth?
Gareth: I'm not sure. When is it?
Boy 1: It's the last weekend in April. From the 28th to the 29th.
Gareth: Seaton is quite far from here, isn't it? It'll be expensive to travel there.
Boy 1: Yes. You'll need to stay in a hotel – but we could share a room. There's a group going from our club so your parents don't need to come.
Gareth: Right. Is it a big competition?
Boy 1: Yes. It's for both adults and juniors. We can't play with the adults so we'd be in the under 16 age group.
Gareth: When's the closing date?
Boy 1: You need to send the form by the 30th of this month. It's only the 8th of November today so you've got some time to think about it.
Gareth: Right. What does the winner get, anyway?
Boy 1: It's cash, but I'm not sure how much.

Now listen again

This is the end of Part Four. Now look at Part Five.

🎧 Practice Test 1 Part 5 (page 77)

You will hear a teacher giving some information about a talk at school. Listen and complete each question. You will hear the information twice.

Can you listen, everyone? I've got some information about a special visitor who's coming to the school next Tuesday. I'm sure a lot of you will be interested because this person has been in the newspapers recently. His name's Martin Woolcott. That's W-double O-L-C-O-double T. He's a very well-known

Recording Scripts

explorer, and he's going to talk about his last trip to Antarctica. The talk will be after school from 4.30 to 5.30 p.m. So if you want to come you have to ask your parents to sign the form I'm going to give you. The talk will be held in the school hall. As you know, there isn't enough room there for everyone. We've decided that only 18 out of each class will be able to go. So to be sure of a place you need to fill in the form and give it to me as soon as possible. OK. Any questions?

Now listen again

This is the end of the part five. This is the end of the test.

(38) Practice Test 2 Part 1 (page 88)

This is the Total KET Key English Test Practice Test 2. There are five parts to the test. Parts One, Two, Three, Four and Five. We will now stop for a moment before we start the test.
Please ask any questions now because you must NOT speak during the test.

Now look at the instructions for Part One.

You will hear five short conversations. You will hear each conversation twice. There is one question for each conversation. For each question, choose the right answer, A, B or C. Here is an example:
What time does the boy's football match start?
Dad: What time is your football match tomorrow, Isaac?
Issac: I don't think it's until ten, because we're meeting at school at nine o'clock
Dad: And it takes about half an hour to get there.
Issac: Yes, and we'll need time to get ready.

Now listen again

The answer is 10 o'clock so there is a tick in box A. Now we are ready to start.

1 What does the girl need to buy?
  Girl: Mum, I want to make a cake for Sophie's birthday tomorrow.
  Mum: That's fine. But we've only got two eggs. Is that enough?
  Girl: It says four in the cook book so I'll go to the shop and get some more.
  Mum: We've certainly got lots of flour and butter.

Now listen again

2 Where will Chris meet his mum?
  Mum: I'm afraid I can't meet you from school today, Chris?
  Chris: Don't worry, Mum. I want to go to the park with my friends anyway.
  Mum: Ok come home by train and I'll see you at the station. Phone me when you get there.
  Chris: OK.

Now listen again

3 What has Sasha borrowed?
  Girl 1: I love your dress, Sasha.
  Sasha: Thanks. I got it in a sale last week.
  Girl 1: Are the shoes and bag new too?
  Sasha: Oh, the shoes aren't mine. They're Chloe's. She said I could wear them. And the bag's quite old.

Now listen again

4 Which train ticket does the boy decide to get?
  Boy: Can I buy a ticket to Grafton, please?
  Man: If you travel after 9.30, it's cheaper. The tickets are only £5.35 but if you buy one now it's £7.80.
  Boy: OK. I'll wait. Last time I'm sure I only paid £4.20.
  Man: I'm afraid the prices have just gone up.

Now listen again

5 What time does the library shut today?
  Girl: Will the library be open at half past five today?
  Man: Yes. It's open until quarter to six every day except Wednesday.
  Girl: What time does it close then?
  Man: At 5 o'clock. Because we have a staff meeting then.

Now listen again

This is the end of Part One. Now look at Part Two.

(39) Practice Test 2 Part 2 (page 89)

Listen to Ryan talking to his mother about a school trip to the city. Where did Ryan go each day? For questions 6-10, write a letter A-H next to each day. You will hear the conversation twice.

Mum: So Ryan, tell me what you did each day.
Ryan: Well, on Monday it was a nice day so we went to the zoo. It was really big.
Mum: What did you do on Tuesday?
Ryan: That was a good day, too. We went to where John Hart used to live. He wrote lots of plays. It was very close to the river.
Mum: That sounds interesting. Did you go to any museums?
Ryan: Yes. On Wednesday we went to the Museum of Modern Art – we tried to copy some of the paintings.
Mum: Really?
Ryan: Yes. Mine weren't very good. And the next day, on Thursday, we went and learned about the history of medicine at another museum. That was a bit boring.
Mum: What did you on Friday?
Ryan: On Friday we saw The Star Ship. It was really good. It's a very popular show. The theatre was so crowded.
Mum: Did you have time for any shopping?
Ryan: Some of the girls did that on Saturday but I played football in the park instead. And after lunch we came home.

Now listen again

This is the end of Part Two. Now look at Part Three.

59

🎧 Practice Test 2 Part 3 (page 90)

Listen to Jade talking to her friend Oscar about her favourite sport. For each question, choose the right answer (A, B or C). You will hear each conversation twice.

Oscar: Hi Jade. What have you got in that shopping bag?
Jade: Oh hello, Oscar. It's just a hat for skiing. I saw some beautiful jackets and boots but they were too expensive.
Oscar: When did you start skiing?
Jade: I started when I was nine. My brother was only five – he was too young. Seven is the best age to start.
Oscar: Can everyone in your family ski?
Jade: Yes. My mum's always skied. She's still the fastest. But my brother's getting faster. My dad's OK – not brilliant.
Oscar: Do you go every year?
Jade: Mmmm. We mostly go in the holidays in December but I prefer February when it's a bit warmer. January's good too because it's not so crowded.
Oscar: Have you ever had an accident?
Jade: I've never broken anything. But two years ago I fell off a ski lift onto my back. It was lucky it wasn't my head. I didn't have to go to hospital though.
Oscar: Where do you ski?
Jade: Yes. We love Austria and we've been once to Canada. But I'd like to try Argentina because you can ski there in July.

Now listen again.

This is the end of Part Three. Now look at Part Four.

🎧 Practice Test 2 Part 4 (page 91)

You will hear a boy, Adam, asking a teacher for information about a running race. Listen and complete each question. You will hear the conversation twice.

Adam: Excuse me, Mr Williams. Can I ask you some questions about the running race? I didn't get the letter about it.
Mr Williams: Yes, Adam. It's for everyone in the lower school
Adam: Right. And I heard it's on the 15th of November. Is that right?
Mr Williams: There was a football match on that day so it was moved from the 15th to the 25th.
Adam: OK. What time is it?
Mr Williams: Well, the race doesn't start until 2.30 but you need to have lunch at 12.30 so you've got time to practise before the race.
Adam: Sure. Someone told me we have to run 10 kilometres.
Mr Williams: This is the first race so it's only five, but we want you all to do 10 kilometres next June.
Adam: I see. Where are we actually going to run to?
Mr Williams: We'll run from school to Tyrone Farm.
Adam: Sorry, could you spell that, please?
Mr Williams: Yes. It's T-Y-R-O-N-E. Don't worry. You won't get lost. There'll be lots of boys running with you.
Adam: How many?
Mr Williams: 465.
Adam: That's a lot!

Now listen again

This is the end of Part Four. Now look at Part Five.

🎧 Practice Test 2 Part 5 (page 91)

You will hear a girl leaving a message for a friend. Listen and complete each question. You will hear the information twice.

Hi, this is Stella. I just wanted to check you know how to get to my house. So you know it's Bridge Street, OK? I live in a large apartment building. You can't miss it, it's the only one in the street. I live at number 46. There are actually four buildings there so you need to find the entrance for apartments 35-50. I'm on the fifth floor so it's best to take the lift.
OK. So to get to my apartment you need to take the 65 bus and get off at the stop outside the park gate. From there cross the road and go straight ahead at the traffic lights. After about 50 metres you'll see a cinema on the right. Turn left there and that's my street.
I'll give you my phone number at home, so you can call me on that if you need to. It's 0307 912208. Or call me on my mobile.
See you later. Bye.

Now listen again.

This is the end of the part five. This is the end of the test.

Extra Activities

UNIT 1 – What do you do every day?

1. Write one thing you do each day.
2. In pairs tell your partner what you do, e.g. *On Mondays I go swimming at 4 p.m.*
3. What do you both do? Find out if you do any of the same things.

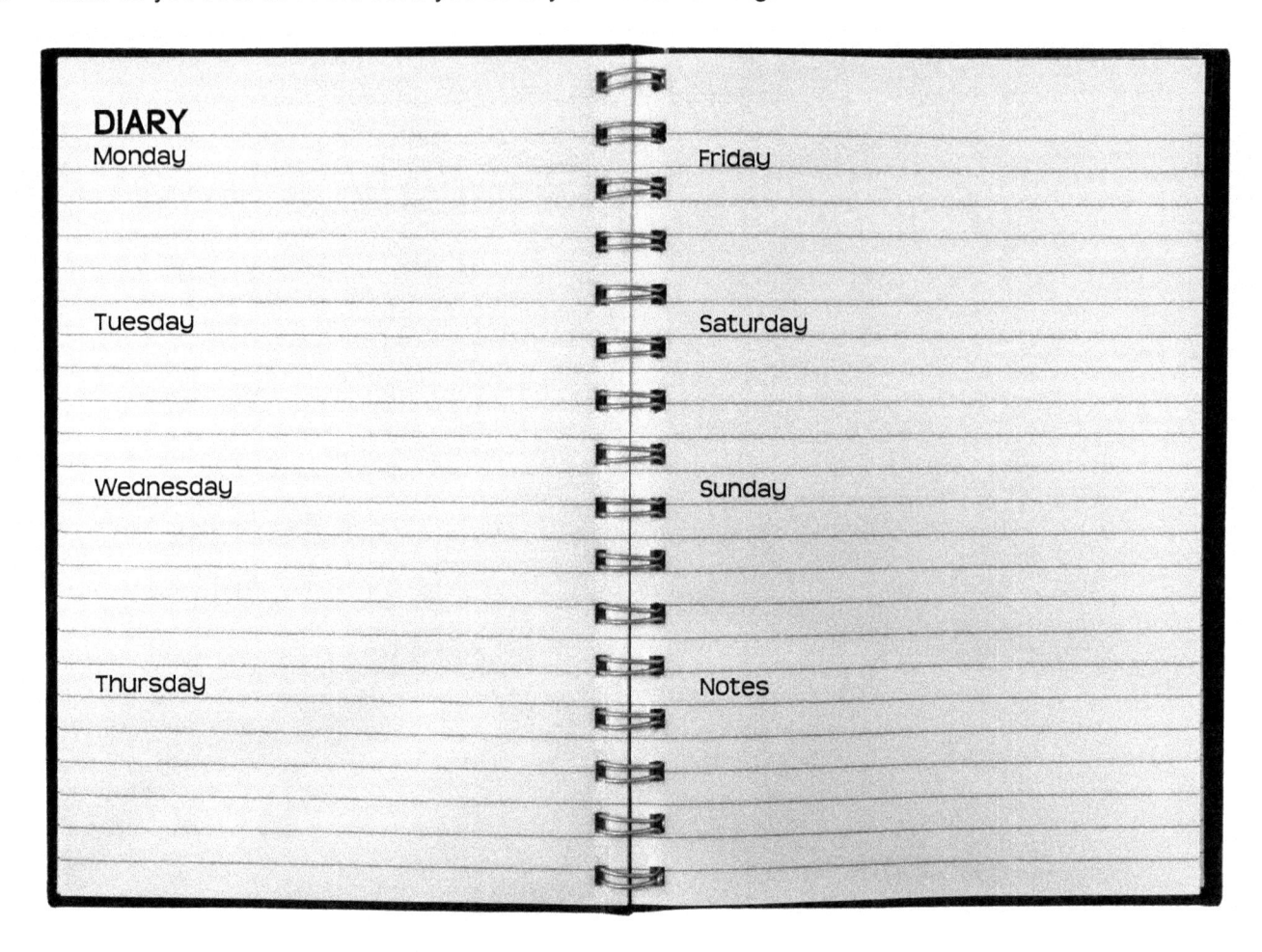

DIARY

Monday

Tuesday

Wednesday

Thursday

Friday

Saturday

Sunday

Notes

Teacher's notes

1. Ask learners to write one thing they do for each day and also to write the time, e.g. *Play football at 5.30 p.m.* NB tell them to write something different for each day.
2. Learners tell their partner what they do each day. With a strong class learners can ask questions to find out what their partner does every day. 'What do you do on Monday? What time do you ...?' (although the Present Simple question forms aren't introduced until unit 2). They write what their partner does in the second diary. Drill the questions and demonstrate the activity in open class. They should find something they both do on the same day.
3. Feedback: elicit sentences, e.g. *On Monday we both watch (name of TV programme) at 8.30.*

Extra Activities

UNIT 2 – Your family

1 Draw your family here.
2 Write their names.
3 Then answer the questions below.
4 Ask and answer the questions with a partner about your families.

I have .... (brothers and sisters) .

My .... name's ....

My .... is called ....

My .... hair is ....

My .... is .... years old.

Teacher's notes

1 Ask learners to draw a picture of their family. If learners don't like drawing, they can do a family tree instead. You may need to demonstrate this on the board.
2 Learners complete the sentences about people in their family.
3 Pairwork. Learners take turns to describe their family to their partner.
4 Feedback: ask learners a few questions. *How old is your grandmother? How many cousins have you got?'* etc. and correct any common errors from the pairwork.

UNIT 3 – Who...?

1 Go around the class and find someone who likes each of the following.
Find someone who...

	NAME
☺ loves Science.	
☹ hates Languages.	
☺ enjoys sports.	
☺ always walks to school.	
☺ is good at Art.	
☺ has a music lesson once a week.	
☺ usually gets up early on Sunday.	
☺ goes to the library in break times.	

Teacher's notes

1 Before learners do the mingle, elicit the question forms with the class and drill. *Do you love Science?* and the response. *Yes, I do. No, I don't.* Check they aren't saying *Do you loves Science?* Explain they need to find one person who loves Science, etc. and write a name in each box.

2 Tell the class to stand up and talk to at least eight other people.

3 Feedback: ask a learner, *Who loves Science?* etc. and they say the name of the person they found who loves Science.

4 Extension activity: get the class to make a pie chart of the class's favourite subjects. Do a ranking activity where each learner numbers a list of subjects in order of preference. Collate the information on the board with the whole class. Learners then produce the chart in small groups.

PHOTOCOPIABLE © 2010 Black Cat Publishing

Extra Activities

UNIT 4 – What are they doing?

1. Cut out the cards, mix them and turn them over.
2. In pairs turn over two cards and say what the people are doing.
3. Find pairs of cards.
4. The winner is the person with the most pairs.

Teacher's notes

1. Have learners work in pairs or small groups. They should cut out the cards and shuffle them before turning them over to make a 4 x 4 square. (You may want to consider sticking the cards on coloured paper or cardboard before to make them stronger.)
2. Learners then take turns to turn over two of the cards at a time. They should say what the people are doing each time. They must try to remember where the photos are so they can match pairs.
3. Extension activity: get students to make more cards on their own, either by drawing the activities or by bringing in pictures from magazines. As a variation the students could try to match one picture card with the another where the action is written.

PHOTOCOPIABLE © 2010 Black Cat Publishing

UNIT 5 – Which sport is...?

1. Look at the pictures below and write the name of each sport.
2. In pairs discuss and answer the questions.
3. Compare your answers as a class.

A	B	C	D
E	F	G	H
I	J	K	L

Which sport is...

1. the easiest to learn?
2. the most boring to watch on TV?
3. the most dangerous?
4. the most exciting to watch on TV?
5. the most difficult to learn?
6. the most expensive to do?
7. Which sport would you most like to learn?
8. Which sport would you least like to learn?

You   Your partner

Teacher's notes

1. In pairs learners label the pictures and discuss the questions.
2. Then they have ask and answer the questions and complete the table with either the letter or name of the sport.
3. Orally do a quick comparison of all the learners' answers. Ask for reasons why.

KEY **A** basketball **B** swimming **C** hockey **D** golf **E** mountain climbing **F** skiing **G** baseball **H** tennis **I** high jump **J** running **K** football (AmE soccer) **L** volleyball

PHOTOCOPIABLE © 2010 Black Cat Publishing

Extra Activities

UNIT 6 – Which food...?

1 Look at the pictures and in pairs or small groups ask and answer the questions below.

1 Which of these foods do you like? Which don't you like?
....
2 Which ones do you have for breakfast? Which ones for lunch or dinner?
....
3 Which ones do you eat with a knife and fork and which ones do you eat with your hands?
....
4 Which ones are sweet and which ones are savoury?
....
5 Which are the three healthiest? Which are the three unhealthiest?
....

Teacher's notes

1 Check orally that learners recognise all the foods in the pictures. Explain any unfamiliar vocabulary in the questions, especially *sweet* and *savoury*.
2 Learners should work through the questions in pairs or small groups.
3 Feedback: ask some of the students to tell the class their answers. Compare answers amongst the groups and discuss similarities and differences.

PHOTOCOPIABLE © 2010 Black Cat Publishing

UNIT 7 – When did you...?

1   Think of the last time you went on holiday. Complete these questions using the Past Simple. Then, in pairs, answer the questions.

   A   Where .... you go?   ....
   B   How old .... you?   ....
   C   What .... you like about it?   ....

2   Now ask and answer the three questions about the things in the table.

	You	Your partner
your first journey by plane		
your first visit to another country		
your first time away from home		
the first time you rode a bicycle		
the last time you went in a taxi		

Teacher's notes

1   Learners complete the questions and ask and answer them in pairs.
2   Give them time to make notes under the YOU column before they ask and answer the questions with a partner.
3   Feedback: correct any errors and ask some learners to give some information about their partner.

Extra Activities

UNIT 8 – You shouldn't...

1 Look at the symbols on page 41 of the Student's Book and then make some safety signs for your school/classroom. Draw pictures and write the message using one of the modal verbs below. Cut them out and place them in appropriate places.

You must...   You mustn't...   You should...   You shouldn't...

....

Teacher's notes

You will need coloured pens/pencils and scissors.

1 Elicit some ideas for the class about rules in different areas of the school, e.g. *playground, cafe, classroom, science lab*, etc.
2 In groups learners can design their own safety signs.
3 Cut out the safety signs for each group and put them on the classroom walls. The class can walk around and read them. They could vote on the best sign.
4 Keep any useful/relevant signs displayed in the classroom.

UNIT 9 – What are they wearing?

1   Look at the photos in pairs or in small groups and describe what each person is wearing.

1 What are the people wearing?

Person 1 ....

Person 2 ....

Person 3 ....

Person 4 ....

Person 5 ....

Teacher's notes

1   In pairs/small groups learners describe the clothes in as much detail as possible.
2   Check they are ordering the adjectives correctly.
3   Feedback: correct any errors and ask some learners to tell the class their answers.

Extra Activities

Unit 10 – Let's have a party

1. Organise a party with a partner.
   Decide:
   - what the party is for
   - where it is
   - what time it is
   - what food you want to have
   - if people need to wear special clothes
   - if people need to bring anything

2. Design your invitation

3. Then invite your friends to your party.

PARTY!

DAY: ....

TIME: ....

PLACE: ....

Teacher's notes

You will need pens, coloured pens and scissors.

1. Ask learners to tell you about any parties they have been to recently. Explain that they are going to organise their own party.
2. Divide the class into pairs. Hand out coloured pens and tell them to design their invitation.
3. Elicit the language of invitations. *We're having a party next... Would you like to come? Yes, I'd love to. No, sorry I can't. I'm going to X's party.*
4. Get some learners to invite you to their party as a demonstration. Ask questions *What time is it? What should I wear? Do I need to bring anything?*
5. Learners stand up and walk around inviting other learners to their party.

PHOTOCOPIABLE © 2010 Black Cat Publishing

Unit 11 – How many times?

1 Complete the questions and then find out how many/how many times your classmates have done these things this week/month/year.

Questions	Name:	Name:
How many books/read/this month?		
How many times/been to the beach/this year?		
How many parties/been/this year?		
How many times/been/cinema/this month?		
How many pizzas/eaten/this month?		
How many times/washed the dishes/this week?		
How many times/been/late for school/this year?		
How many times/travelled by plane/this year?		
..............................?		
..............................?		

Teacher's notes

1 Elicit the questions: *How many parties have you been to this year?* etc. Elicit the answers: *I've been to three parties. How many times have you washed the dishes this week? Once, twice, three times,* etc., *none*.

2 Learners ask and answer in groups of three.

3 Feedback: find out who has done these things the most often.

Extra Activities

Unit 12 – For sale

1 Prepare an advert of something that belongs to you that you want to sell. Include as much information as you can about it, e.g. *colour, age*, etc.
2 Then try and sell it to someone in the class.

FOR SALE

Teacher's notes

1 Ask the class if they/their parents ever buy anything on online or from second-hand shops/markets.
2 Tell the class they are going to try and sell one of their possessions to someone in the class.
   Give the class time to draw a picture of or describe the thing they want to sell. They should include as much information as possible, e.g. *size, colour, how old it is*, etc. and the price they want for it.
3 Elicit useful phrases for buying and selling. *Would you like to buy my...? How much is it? That's too expensive.*
4 Learners can do their buying and selling as a mingle or in groups.
5 Feedback: find out who managed to sell their items and for how much.

Unit 13 – Personality test

1 Take this personality test. Compare answers. Do you agree?

1 Which of these animals do you like best? Put them in order of preference. 1 = your favourite, 4 = your least favourite.

2 What do you think of when you see these photos? Write one word for each one.

3 Think of a person you know well for each of the colours below.

yellow   *orange*   *red*   *green*

....

Teacher's notes

1 Get learners to complete the test quickly – they shouldn't spend too much time thinking about their answers.
2 Talk to them about what they think the answers mean. Then read or give them the interpretations.
3 Feedback: discuss how accurate they think the test is.

INTERPRETATIONS

1 The order that you choose defines the priorities in your life.
   tiger: pride   **sheep**: love   **horse**: family   **cow**: work

2 the **dog** represents your own personality.
   the **cat** represents your partner's personality.
   the **rat** represents the personality of your enemies.
   the **ocean** represents your own life.

3 **yellow**: someone you will never forget.
   orange: someone you could consider a good friend.
   red: someone you really love.
   green: someone you will remember all your life.

74 PHOTOCOPIABLE © 2010 Black Cat Publishing

Extra Activities

Unit 14 – Relationships

A For each space, read the sentences and write the name of one person.

1 Someone who makes me laugh.
2 Someone who is always kind to me.
3 Someone I don't get on with.
4 The richest person in my family.
5 The youngest person in my family.
6 The coolest person I know.

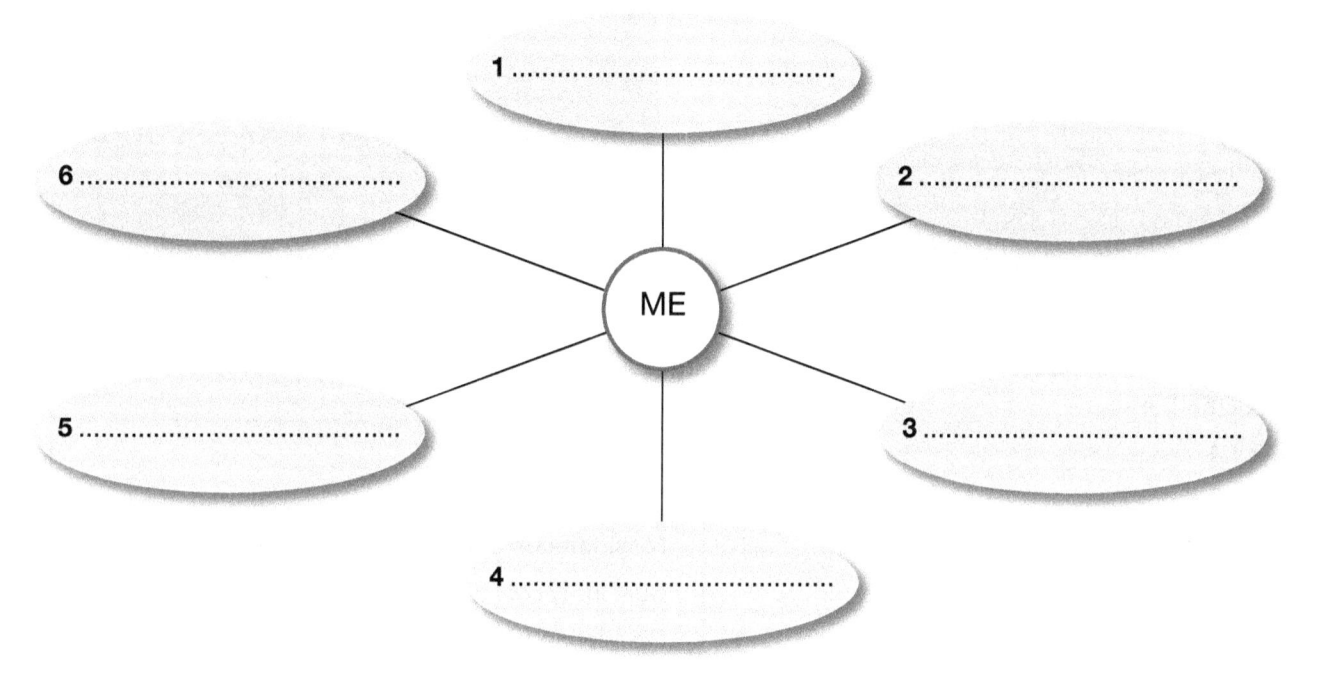

```
        1 ..............................

6 ..........................                    2 ..........................

                    ME

5 ..........................                    3 ..........................

        4 ..............................
```

✂--

B For each space, read the sentences and write the name of one person.

1 The funniest person I know.   ....
2 The cleverest person I know.   ....
3 Someone who makes me angry.   ....
4 The oldest person in my family.   ....
5 Someone who is very shy.   ....
6 Someone who helps me a lot.   ....

Teacher's notes

1 Cut out the spidergram and sentences. Divide learners into As & Bs. Tell them to read the sentences and write the name of one person for each sentence in the box. Give them a few minutes to do this silently.
2 In pairs learners ask and answer about the names in the boxes, e.g. *Who is Maria? Why did you write her name there? What's David like?*
3 Feedback: ask learners who have performed well to describe one person for the class.

PHOTOCOPIABLE © 2010 Black Cat Publishing   75

Unit 15 – City factfiles

1   In pairs ask and answer questions to complete the missing information in the factfiles about the two cities in the pictures below.

CITY 1

CITY 2

STUDENT A	STUDENT B
CITY 1	**CITY 1**
City: **Bangkok**	City: ....
Most famous building:	Most famous building: **The Grand Palace**
Built in:	Built in: **1782**
Population of city: **9 million**	Population of city: ....
Name of river:	Name of river: **Chao Praya**
CITY 2	**CITY 2**
City:	City: **Prague**
Most famous building: **St Vitus Cathedral**	Most famous building: ....
Built in:	Built in: **14th century**
Population of city: **1.3 million**	Population of city: ....
Name of river: **Vltava**	Name of river: ....

Teacher's notes

1   Divide class into pairs. Give each learner either worksheet A or B. Tell the class not to look at their partner's worksheet.
2   Explain they need to find the missing information on their worksheet by asking their partner questions. Elicit the questions learners need to ask, e.g. *Which city is this? What's the most famous building?*
3   Learners ask and answer in pairs.
4   Feedback: find out if any learners have visited these cities and which they would prefer to visit. As a follow up learners could do an internet search to find out more information about either Prague or Bangkok.

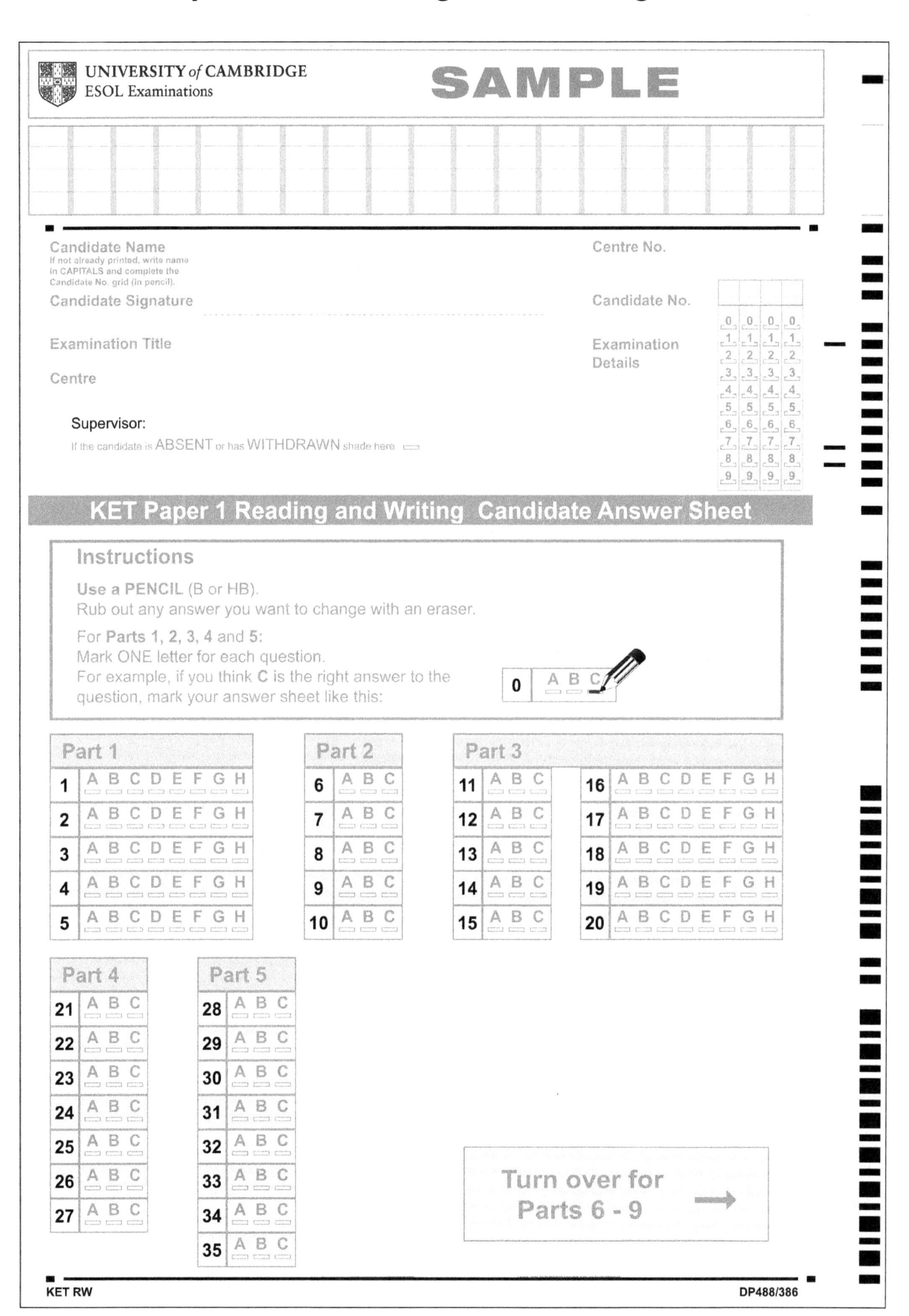

Paper 1 – Reading and Writing Answer Sheet

UNIVERSITY of CAMBRIDGE
ESOL Examinations

SAMPLE

Candidate Name
If not already printed, write name in CAPITALS and complete the Candidate No. grid (in pencil).

Candidate Signature

Examination Title

Centre

Supervisor:
If the candidate is ABSENT or has WITHDRAWN shade here

Centre No.

Candidate No.

Examination Details

KET Paper 1 Reading and Writing Candidate Answer Sheet

Instructions

Use a **PENCIL** (B or HB).
Rub out any answer you want to change with an eraser.

For **Parts 1, 2, 3, 4** and **5**:
Mark ONE letter for each question.
For example, if you think **C** is the right answer to the question, mark your answer sheet like this:

0 A B C

Part 1
1 A B C D E F G H
2 A B C D E F G H
3 A B C D E F G H
4 A B C D E F G H
5 A B C D E F G H

Part 2
6 A B C
7 A B C
8 A B C
9 A B C
10 A B C

Part 3
11 A B C
12 A B C
13 A B C
14 A B C
15 A B C

16 A B C D E F G H
17 A B C D E F G H
18 A B C D E F G H
19 A B C D E F G H
20 A B C D E F G H

Part 4
21 A B C
22 A B C
23 A B C
24 A B C
25 A B C
26 A B C
27 A B C

Part 5
28 A B C
29 A B C
30 A B C
31 A B C
32 A B C
33 A B C
34 A B C
35 A B C

Turn over for Parts 6 - 9 →

KET RW   DP488/386

Paper 1 – Reading and Writing Answer Sheet

SAMPLE

For **Parts 6, 7 and 8**:

Write your answers in the spaces next to the numbers (36 to 55) like this:

| 0 | example |

Part 6

		Do not write here
36		1 36 0
37		1 37 0
38		1 38 0
39		1 39 0
40		1 40 0

Part 7

		Do not write here
41		1 41 0
42		1 42 0
43		1 43 0
44		1 44 0
45		1 45 0
46		1 46 0
47		1 47 0
48		1 48 0
49		1 49 0
50		1 50 0

Part 8

		Do not write here
51		1 51 0
52		1 52 0
53		1 53 0
54		1 54 0
55		1 55 0

Part 9 (Question 56): Write your answer below.

Do not write below (Examiner use only)

0 1 2 3 4 5

78 PHOTOCOPIABLE © 2010 Black Cat Publishing – Reproduced with the kind permission of Cambridge ESOL

Paper 2 – Listening Answer Sheet

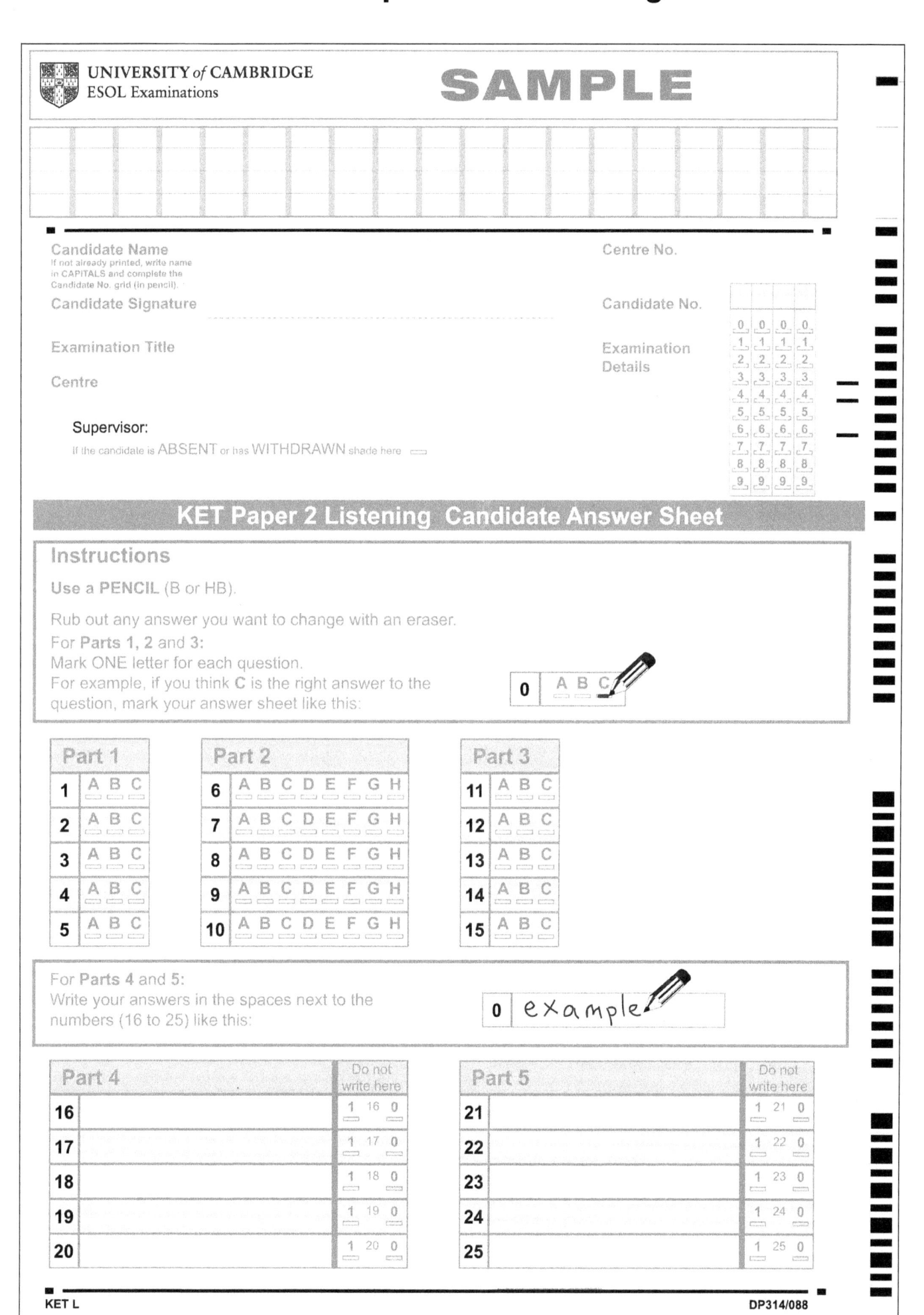

BLACK CAT

Internet: www.blackcat-cideb.com
email: info@blackcat-cideb.com

Editors: Victoria Bradshaw, Joanna Burgess
Book and cover design: Nadia Maestri, Maura Santini
Page layout: Maura Santini
Design coordinator: Simona Corniola
Picture research: Laura Lagomarsino

Art Director: Nadia Maestri

© 2010 Black Cat, Genoa, London

First edition: March 2010

Every effort has been made to trace the copyright holders and we apologise in advance for any unintentional omissions. We would be pleased to insert the appropriate acknowledgement in any subsequent edition of this publication.
All rights reserved. No part of this publication may be reproduced, stored in a retrieval system, or transmitted, in any form or by any means, electronic, mechanical, photocopying, recording or otherwise, without the previous written permission of the publisher.
The publisher reserves the right to concede authorisation for the reproduction of up to 15% of this publication upon payment of the established fee. All requests for such authorisation should be forwarded to AIDRO (Associazione Italiana per i Diritti di Riproduzione delle Opere dell'Ingegno), corso di Porta Romana, 108 – 20122 Milano – email segreteria@aidro.org; www.aidro.org

In accordance with DL 74/92, the use of any commercial brand images and/or logos in this text is purely illustrative and should in no way be interpreted as endorsement on the part of Cideb Black Cat Publishing of such products and/or brands.

Printed in Italy by Rotolito Lombarda, Seggiano di Pioltello (MI)

Reprint	II	III	IV	V	VI
Year	2013	2014	2015	2016	2017